«Δύναμη και Παράδοση » Strength and Tradition: History
and Memory of the Greek Genocide in Turkey and its
Impact on Culture and Heritage in the United States

by
Elenie Louvaris

This thesis for the Master of Arts degree by
Elenie Louvaris
has been approved for the
History Program
by

Rebecca Hunt, Chair
William Wagner
Michael Kozakowski

Date: *May 12, 2018*

Abstract

From 1913-1924 the ethnic-Greeks of Asia Minor were the victims of genocide perpetrated first by agents of the failing Ottoman State, the rise of the Young Turks and finally Mustafa Kemal's Turkish Republic. This study analyzes the actions and effects of the Turks in three sections. The first chapter defines genocide and ethnic cleansing, and gives a historiography of nationalism, the Greek Genocide and includes a brief historical context. The Second chapter contextualizes the atrocities committed in Asia Minor. This is done by first presenting how nationalism transformed the Balkan Peninsula, and then showing how the Turks systematically dismantled Greek communities in Turkey through attacks. Using survivor testimonies from Nicomedia I show that these attacks were committed against the Greek Orthodox Church, clergy as well as women and children purposefully. Further, I endeavor to show that all of these actions were committed against Greeks in an effort to destroy their sense of identity, to sever community ties, and ultimately to remove them from Turkey. In the third and final chapter, I show how despite their efforts, the descendants of the victims of genocide have, in the United States, established institutions, societies, and organizations to perpetuate and preserve the unique culture and identity that the Turks tried so hard to destroy.

The form and content of this abstract are approved. I recommend its publication.
Approved: Rebecca Hunt

DEDICATION

For my γιαγια, Helen Mavromatis.
May the memories of our ancestors be eternal.
Σ'αγαπω.

TABLE OF CONTENTS

CHAPTER

CHAPTER I
INTRODUCTION

On June 23, 1920, Pavlos Balidis rose early, with the intention of calling all the men of the village Fulzaik to harvest their wheat crops.[1] As he stepped out of the door, he "heard [the] loud galloping of a cavalry going down the cobblestoned streets of the agora."[2] He peered down the street and saw "roughly 30 armed Turkish villagers on horseback…[and] at the entrance to the market place…saw the regular army and the gendarmerie descending" from nearby villages.[3] Concerned, Balidis made his way to the coffee house in the center of town to find out what all the commotion was all about. By five o'clock in the evening, Balidis found himself, along with "300 other men and boys," locked inside the church of St. George.[4] Once he realized that they were locked in, Balidis made his way to the edge of the crowd to peer through the cracks in the church doors. There he saw Kemalists "pouring petrol on the doors"—within seconds, both the church and the rest of

---

[1] Fulazik, modern day Fulacik, In the Nicomedia (modern day Izmit) Region of Turkey.
[2] Kostas Faltaits, *The Genocide of the Greeks in Turkey: Survivor Testimonies From The Nicomedia (Izmit) Massacres of 1920-1921*, ed. Ellene Phoufas-Jousma and Aris Tsilfidis (River Vale, NJ, 2016), 43.
The translation and publication of these primary sources are the first available in English. It is the only collection of first hand accounts, that I have found, that were conducted at the time that the genocide was occurring. Most other interviews or accounts were held many years later. For this reason, they will be my main source base in Chapter II.
[3] Testimony of Pavlos Balidis, "Fulazik," in Faltaits, 43.
[4] Testimony of Pavlos Balidis, "Fulazik," in Faltaits, 48.

the buildings in the village were engulfed in flames.[5] Balidis, along with the other men inside the church, broke down the door amidst the flames that would soon consume them. Once freed from the burning church the villagers attempted to flee, but were met by hand grenades being thrown and the unceasing "brrrrrrr" of bullets being discharged from all directions. In the chaos raging all around, Balidis fell into a ditch—there he remained, crouched in fear. After some time, when he heard "musical instruments being played," he cautiously peered over the edge of the ditch.[6] Shocked, he saw a group of Turks dragging "Father Phillipos....with a rope that had been tied around his neck," across the village.[7] All the while, the gunfire continued…and the "shouting and crying and the singing didn't stop either."[8]

Pavlos Balidis and many other ethnic-Greeks in Turkey like him suffered similarly during the Genocide of Greeks in Turkey from 1914-1923.[9] While Baliadis' story is unique in his experience, sadly it is not unique in its brutality. Over

---

[5] Testimony of Pavlos Balidis, "Fulazik," in Faltaits, 48.

The term "Kemalists" refers to either regular or irregular soldiers of the Turkish Republic, led by Mustafa "Atatürk" Kemal, who helped proliferate and establish the nationalist ideology that created modern Turkey. This will be discussed further in coming sections.

[6] Testimony of Pavlos Balidis, "Fulazik," in Faltaits, 50.

[7] Testimony of Pavlos Balidis, "Fulazik," in Faltaits, 50.

[8] Testimony of Pavlos Balidis, "Fulazik," in Faltaits, 50.

[9] For the duration of this paper I will use "the genocide of the Greeks" or "Greek Genocide" to refer to "the genocide of the Greeks in Turkey from 1914-1923." It should also be noted that the phrase "in Turkey" should be assumed to mean "in Turkey during the Genocide of the Greeks from 1914-1923." Additionally, some sources cite the genocide as beginning as early as 1912 and ending sooner than 1923— I have chosen the date range of 1914-1923 as it is the date range endorsed by the International Association for Genocide Scholars.

the almost ten years of forced deportation, death marches, mass killings and torture by the Turks, approximately 1-1.5 million Pontic and Anatolian Greeks were killed.[10]

11

By analyzing victim accounts, such as Balidis,' scholars can specifically analyze the experience of the Greek minority during the Greek Genocide. By looking more deeply into the various minority groups that were a part of this tragic historical event, including Armenians and Assyrians in addition to Anatolian and Pontic Greeks,

---

[10] Tessa Hofmann, "Γενοκτονία Εν Ροή: Cumulative Genocide The Massacres and Deportations of the Greek Population of the Ottoman Empire (1912-1923)," in *The Genocide of the Ottoman Greeks: Studies in State-Sponsored Campaign of Extermination of the Christians of Asia Minor, 1912-1922 and Its Aftermath: History, Law, Memory* (Aristide D. Caratzas, 2011), 109.

[11] *Map of Asia Minor and Pontos*, Maps of Pontos and Pontic Region, http://www.angelfire.com/folk/pontian_net/map.html, accessed March 2018.
Asia Minor and Anatolia are used interchangeably throughout this paper. They both refer to the westernmost region of modern Turkey that is bordered by the Black Sea to the north, the Mediterranean Sea to the south and the Aegean Sea to the West. Pontos or Pontus is a both a region and a distinct Greek sub-culture in northern Asia Minor with villages in the mountains and coast bordering the Black Sea.

scholars can more accurately discuss the similarities and differences of their experience while also preserving a more complete memory of those who suffered at the hands of the Turks.

Brief Historical Context

The genocide of the Greeks in Turkey can be seen as the culmination of age old tensions between the Greeks and Turks dating back to the fall of the Byzantine and rise of the Ottoman Empire. As a result, Greece and Turkey found themselves on opposing sides of a number of wars including: the First Balkan War (October 1912-May 1913), the Second Balkan War (June 1913), World War I and the Greek-Turkish War (Asia Minor War, 1920-1922). By the time the Greeks entered WWI in 1917, persecutions of Ottoman non-Muslim populations (mostly Armenian and Greek) were already taking place.[12] Nationalist ideas were present in both Greece and the Ottoman Empire (later the Turkish Republic) and resulted in violence and persecutions of both ethnic-Greeks, and to a smaller extent, Muslim-Turks in Anatolia.

In Greece, irredentist nationalist Elefterios Venizelos pushed for the reincorporation of lands deemed to be historically tied to ancient Greek civilizations. Simultaneously, in the declining Ottoman Empire the Young Turks led by the Three Pashas (Talaat Pasha, Enver Pasha and Dejmal Pasha) established a nationalist policy of Turkification in order to create a core Muslim state that would remain loyal to the Turkish state and not outside forces—like Greeks who if allowed to remain in the country would continue to serve as indigenous resources

---

[12] John Mourelos, "The 1914 Persecutions of Greeks in the Ottoman Empire and the First Attempt at an Exchange of Minorities between Greece and Turkey," in Hofmann, Bjørnlund, and Meichanetsidis, 113–36.

for enemies of the Turkish republic."[13] The decision to become a homogenous Turkish Muslim country resulted in the removal and/or reduction of the Christian minority population.[14] Ultimately, this resulted in the genocide of Anatolian and Pontic Greeks as well as Armenians and Assyrians throughout the Turkish interior and Asia Minor.[15]

   The genocide of the Greeks should be understood as a culmination of events that ultimately resulted in atrocity, rather than as something that occurred in a vacuum. It was the result of nationalist policies in both Greece and Turkey as well as a result of Western European interference in Balkan/South Eastern European politics and relations. Despite this, the atrocities perpetrated by the Turks against non-Muslim Christian minorities is important to the understanding of the creation of a homogenous Turkey. It is for this reason that I utilize the primary source testimonies documented by Kostas Faltaits in order to show how Greek communities were dismantled in Asia Minor through attacks on their religious institutions, religious leaders, and

---

[13] Norman M. Naimark, *Fires of Hatred: Ethnic Cleansing in Twentieth-Century Europe* (Cambridge, MA: Harvard University Press, 2001), 189.

[14] Uğur Ümit Üngör, *The Making of Modern Turkey: Nation and State in Eastern Anatolia, 1913-1950* (Oxford: Oxford University Press, 2011).
For a more detailed explanation of both Greek and Turkish nationalism and relations, please refer to chapter 2.

[15] While Pontic Greeks are officially recognized as a group that suffered separately from Anatolian Greeks by IAGS, and have been/will be mentioned in this paper, I do not endeavor here to study them as a separate group. In the analysis of primary source material I will draw conclusions that are to reflect on the destruction of religion/language/culture/heritage that Greeks, both Anatolian and Pontic, suffered. That being said, in the latter part of my argument when discussing preservation of culture and heritage in the U.S., I will use those dedicated specifically to Pontos as a reflection of Asia Minor as a whole.

on their women and children. Through this analysis I endeavor to show how Turks employed genocidal violence to force ethnic-Greek disassociation of community and identity to force them out of the country. Finally, in chapter three, I will show how despite the violence endured, Greeks of Asia Minor have preserved their unique culture and identity in the United States.

Historiography

As a newer topic that offers few scholarly works
that pertain specifically to the Greek genocide, a widening
of the scope was necessary to gain a better idea of what was
and was not being discussed and why. For this reason the
historiography of the Greek genocide encompasses works
of scholars that study nationalism, genocide in general, the
Armenian genocide, ethnic cleansing, and the Balkan
Peninsula. In this broader historiographic lens the Greek
genocide is very rarely discussed specifically. If it is, it is
mentioned in passing and/or deemed an ethnic cleansing
(not a genocide). This is largely due to the debate that
continues between scholars on the aforementioned
terminology, and because of the politicized nature of the
topic itself. For this reason in the few works that are
dedicated to the Greek genocide a significant portion of
each study first defines the Greek genocide as a genocide
and not an ethnic cleansing before delving into other
arguments. First, we must consider the trends and theories
discussed in the scholarship of nationalism in order to
begin to understand how populations of people that
coexisted for centuries so quickly turned to crimes against
humanity in the name their nation-state.

Broadly speaking, the shift in loyalties from local to
national happened due to the dissemination of nationalist
ideas and rhetoric over time. Nationalism, as a modern
concept of state building, is considered by scholars like
Muhammad Badiul Alam, to have begun with the French
Revolution (1789). These scholars maintain that when

French King Louis XVI was decapitated all loyalties, despite class differences, were sworn to the national state rather than to the monarchy.[16] The ideals espoused in France were further developed and expressed in Germany during their unification and creation of the German nation. Thus, nationalism was able to increasingly gain "broad popular support" first in Europe, and eventually throughout the world.[17] As nationalism spread it took on a variety of forms and is expressed in a six-fold classification referred to as the Hayes Formula. Carlton J. H. Hayes lists the following—humanitarian nationalism, Jacobin nationalism, liberal nationalism, integral nationalism and economic nationalism—as the six classifications.[18]

As with many ideological concepts nationalism does not have one universally accepted definition, and there are a variety of types of nationalism that shape what individual scholars deem nationalism to be. That being said and in the most general sense,

> Nationalism is the group consciousness that breeds a sentiment of unity, a feeling of oneness and likemindedness [sic] among themselves. It denotes a people's sense of collective destiny through a common past and the vision of a common future. It gives each nation its own distinct personality different from all other nations of the world which

---

[16] Muhammad Badiul Alam, "Contemporary Ideas and Theories of Nationalism," *The Indian Journal of Political Science* 41, no. 3 (September 1980): 368.

[17] Badiul Alam, 368.

[18] Badiul Alam, 369; Carlton J. H. Hayes, *The Historical Evolution of Modern Nationalism* (New York: R.R. Smith, 1931).

also helps in creating a state of mind among the individuals that inspires their loyalty to the nation.[19]

Rogers Brubraker extends the understanding of nationalism with his concept of "groupism."
Groupism is explained as the tendency "to treat various categories of people as if they were internally homogenous, externally bounded groups, even unitary collective actors with common purposes; and to take ethnic and racial groups and nations as basic constituents of social life, chief protagonists of social conflicts and fundamental units of social analysis."[20] This theory of groupism has persisted despite other research, such as that of Max Weber, that challenges the idea that humanity is separated into discrete races that are tightly bound and unchanging.[21] This challenge has led more recently to research which espouses the idea of groupness as "a variable, not a constant" that varies both across and within "putative groups."[22] These changes can occur in different forms which include "reputational cascades" (Timur Kuran), "identity cascades" (David Laitin), and "language shifts" (Abram de Swann).[23]

---

[19] Badiul Alam, 373.
[20] Rogers Brubaker, "Ethnicity, Race, and Nationalism," *Annual Review of Sociology* 35 (2009): 28.
[21] Max Weber, *Economy and Society* (Berkeley: University of California Press, 1978), 385–359; 922–26.
[22] Brubaker, "Ethnicity, Race, and Nationalism," 28–30.
[23] Brubaker, 31; Timur Kuran, "Ethnic Norms and Their Transformation through Reputational Cascades," *Journal of Legal Studies* 27 (1998): 623–59; David D. Laitin, *Identitiy in Formation: The Russian-Speaking Populations in the Near Abroad* (Ithaca, NY: Cornell University Press, 1998); David D. Laitin, *Nations, States, and Violence* (New York: Oxford University Press, 2007); Abram de Swaan, "A Political Sociology of the World Language System," *Language Problems and Language Planning* 22, no. 1,2

In the same vein, other scholars such as Brubaker and
Laitin have examined, the methodical projects of group-
making such as "invention of tradition" which establishes
new ideas of group identity by "representing them as
[having] always already [been] there."[24] With this in mind,
nationalism can further be generally separated into two
theories of nationalism, Perennialist or Modernist.

　　Perennialists like Steven Grosby, "stress the
continuities between modern nations and their pre-modern"
ancestors like the Hebrews, the Greeks and the Roman
Empire. Modernists, like Umut Özkirimli, Ernest Gellner
and Nicos Mouzelis, argue for a more "restrictive use of the
term 'nation' as a category exclusive to modernity" and/or
industrialization.[25] While perennialist theory makes
poignant arguments for the connections between ancient
and modern nations, it was not until the sixteenth and
seventeenth century Western Europe that "modern
nationalist states" and ideas began to take shape.[26] It was at

---

(1998): 63–75, 109–28.

Reputational cascades refers to a changing nationalist identification based on what the
community members around them are doing, so as to avoid appearing disloyal. Identity
cascades builds off of Schelling's tipping model and denotes the rapid changes that can
occur from or too different ethnic, national or linguistic groups. Finally, the idea of a
language shift occurs when a particular language is deemed a "hypercollective good" and
thus increases the number of speakers to the point where other languages are
cumulatively deserted and eventual extinction.

[24] Brubaker, "Ethnicity, Race, and Nationalism," 32.

[25] Umut Özkirimli and Steven Grosby, "Nationalism Theory Debate: The Antiquity of
Nations?," *Nations and Nationalism* 13, no. 3 (2007): 523–24; Siniša Malešević, "Did
Wars Make Nation-States in the Balkans?: Nationalisms, Wars and States in the 19th and
Early 20th Century South East Europe," *Journal of Historical Sociology* 25, no. 3
(September 2012): 300–307; Ernest Gellner, *Nations and Nationalism* (Oxford:
Blackwell, 1983); Ernest Gellner, *Nationalism* (London: Pheonix, 1997).

[26] Badiul Alam, "Contemporary Ideas and Theories of Nationalism," 368.

this time that the state "absorbed the loyalties formerly given to the city, region, church, ruler or overlord," which in turn made it the "most powerful political institution."[27] It is for this reason that within the modernist conception of nationalism that there are two resulting theories: integration theory and conflict theory.

Integration theory of nationalism was initially argued by Max Weber and states that nationalism is the "process of bringing together culturally and socially discrete groups into a single territorial unit and the establishment of a national identity within that unit."[28] For the aforementioned process to occur, the society in question must be in the process of modernization so that group organization via increased social communication can occur and ultimately result in the "erosion of primordial loyalties."[29] Differently, conflict theory (not to be confused with the conquest thesis) focuses on the divisions created within societies during modernization. As the process of modernization occurs conflict theory explains that "society becomes structurally differentiated and…groups are…organized along lines of social stratification" which can intensify community inequalities that already existed.[30] As these divisions intensify and particular groups feel that there is an "unacceptable level of inequality in the distribution of valued resources," nationalism emerges.[31]

---

[27] Badiul Alam, 368.
[28] Max Weber, *Nationalism and Social Communication* (1953), in Badiul Alam, 374.
[29] Badiul Alam, 375.
[30] Badiul Alam, 376.
[31] Badiul Alam, 376.

A prominent conception of the modernization theory comes from Ernest Gellner who identified nationalism and continuous economic growth as the two pillars of modernity.[32] Gellner explains that nationalism is linked to the structural changes that must occur as a society transitions from agrarian to industrial. Further, this transition results in a "modular man" that is "highly flexible" that can successfully navigate a "constantly changing social environment."[33] This modular man is the product of industrialization which requires the migration of people into urban centers and creates a need for standardized communication. This need is provided for through state sponsored educational systems which in turn "fosters strong nationalist identifications" and becomes a "cornerstone of a sate's legitimacy."[34] Gellner continues to explain that in an industrial age culture becomes "high culture," and creates a horizontal cultural divide. This divide causes people to identify oneself not with a particular village or strata, but "first and foremost as members of distinct nations."[35] For Gellner, both state-sponsored education and the merging of culture and state are byproducts of both nationalism and industrialization.[36]

Different from the aforementioned theories, the Conquest Thesis first espoused by sociologists Ludwig

---

[32] Malešević, "Did Wars Make Nation-States in the Balkans?: Nationalisms, Wars and States in the 19th and Early 20th Century South East Europe," 305.

[33] Malešević, 305–6.

[34] Malešević, 305–6.

[35] Malešević, 306.

[36] Ernest Gellner, *Nations and Nationalism* (Oxford: Blackwell, 1983); Ernest Gellner, *Nationalism* (London: Pheonix, 1997).

Gumplowicz, Franz Oppenheimer, Gustav Ratzenhofer and later by Otto Hintze, Max Weber and others, emphasizes the role of violence in nation-building rather than nationalism.[37] These scholars all made arguments that linked state making with organized violence, but it was Charles Tilly that made the connection between "war and state explicit."[38] Tilly's key point being that "state making and war making are mutually constitutive" because "war made the state, and the state made war."[39] Tilly goes so far as to say that "modern bureaucratic, centralized and territorialized nation-states" are the result of "protracted warfare and expensive military campaigns"—not nationalism.[40] Tilly explains that by engaging in protracted warfare, a vicious cycle of

> tighter centralization of rule the expansion of the civil service, tax-collecting agencies, exchequers, police forces and judicial systems. As state power grew it threatened the security of their states…embarking on preventative wares thus perpetuating the vicious cycle whereby war-making leads to the state building and state-building leads to more war-making.[41]

---

[37] Malešević, "Did Wars Make Nation-States in the Balkans?: Nationalisms, Wars and States in the 19th and Early 20th Century South East Europe," 302.
[38] Malešević, 302.
[39] Malešević, 302; Charles Tilly, ed., *The Formation of National States in Western Europe* (Princeton: Princeton University Press, 1975); Charles Tilly, "War Making and State Making as Organized Crime," in *Bringing the State Back In*, ed. P Evans, D Rueschemeyer, and T Skocpol (Cambridge: Cambridge University Press, 1985).
[40] Malešević, "Did Wars Make Nation-States in the Balkans?: Nationalisms, Wars and States in the 19th and Early 20th Century South East Europe," 302.
[41] Malešević, 302.

While taking into consideration theories of nationalism, as well as the conquest thesis in understanding the complex nature of the Balkan Peninsula's diverse peoples it is also important to discuss trans-border forms of nationhood and nationalism.

Trans-border forms of nationalism come into play once states establish both communication and transportation infrastructure system that support and establish trans-border ties between communities. The established infrastructure thus "encourage[s] diasporic and transnational modes of identification and organization" prompting new ideas of self-understanding.[42] Trans-border forms of nationalism, multicultural forms of nationalism, national self-understanding, diasporic forms of ethnicity, race, and nationhood are all results of the "diffusion and institutionalization of notions of human rights…[and] multiculturalism" both of which limit models of "unitary and sovereign nation-statehood" identities.[43] The importance of trans-border nationalism is seen in the American descendants of diaspora from Turkey and/or Greece whom are able to claim both American, Greek and/or Turkey based on the internationally established infrastructures that allow for transnational identification. This trans-nationalist identity which does exist in Greek-Americans will be discussed further in Chapter 3, however,

---

[42] Brubaker, "Ethnicity, Race, and Nationalism," 24.
[43] Brubaker, 24.
How these theories of nationalism relate to Greece and the Ottoman Empire/Turkish Republic will be discussed in depth in Chapter 2.

at this point it is important to transition to a discussion of genocide and ethnic cleansing in order to give a more well-rounded understanding of the socio-political climate in the Balkan Peninsula and Turkey at the time.

As an interdisciplinary field, genocide studies offers a wide variety of scholarship explaining what genocide is. By applying field-specific methodologies to particular cases of genocide, scholars attempt to "define…and bound" genocide conceptually to understand its causes and to prevent it from occurring again.[44] The field of genocide studies did not exist until the 1930s when Raphael Lemkin, a scholar consumed with understanding why states killed their own citizens, coined the neologism "genocide."[45] A combination of Greek and Latin roots, genocide means "the intentional destruction of national groups on the basis of their collective identity."[46] As result of international uproar concerning Nazi crimes, in 1948 genocide was defined and declared by the United Nations a "crime under international law" with the passing of the United Nations Convention on the Prevention and Punishment of the Crime of Genocide.[47] Until the passing of the 1948 Convention the field of

---

[44] Adam Jones, *Genocide: A Comprehensive Introduction* (New York: Routledge, 2006), 15.

[45] Steven Leonard Jacobs, "Genocide of Others: Raphael Lemkin, The Genocide of the Greeks, the Holocaust, and the Present Moment," in *The Genocide of the Ottoman Greeks: Studies in State-Sponsored Campaign of Extermination of the Christians of Asia Minor, 1912-1922 and Its Aftermath: History, Law, Memory* (Aristide D. Caratzas, 2011), 297–310.

[46] Jones, *Genocide: A Comprehensive Introduction*, 10.

[47] *United Nations Convention on the Prevention and Punishment of the Crime of Genocide,* United Nations Office on Genocide Prevention and the Responsibility to Protect, http://www.un.org/en/genocideprevention/genocide.html, accessed September 13, 2017.

genocide studies did not exist; therefore, as a product of the twentieth century genocides during this period are the most heavily studied by scholars.[48] Though much of genocide scholarship focuses on the same case studies its interdisciplinary nature has created diversity in the scholarship produced.

The definition set out by the UN 1948 Convention defined what genocide is, what constitutes genocide, how to punish perpetrators of genocide and how to prevent genocide from happening in the future. The convention listed the following acts when "committed with intent to destroy, in whole or in part, a national, ethnical, racial or religious group" as the criterion in Article 2:

a. Killing members of the group;
b. Causing serious bodily or mental harm to members of the group;
c. Deliberately inflicting on the group conditions of life calculated to bring about its physical destruction in whole or in part;
d. Imposing measures intended to prevent births within the group;
e. Forcibly transferring children out of the group to another group.

Further, under Article III of the convention the UN considers the acts of: "genocide; conspiracy to commit

---

[48] Particularly the Jewish Holocaust (1941-1945) and the Stalinist period in the USSR (1917-1953). Other commonly studied topics include the genocides of indigenous peoples, the Armenian genocide (1915-1923), Cambodia and the Khmer Rouge (late 1960s-1970s), and the holocaust in Rwanda (1994).

genocide; direct and public incitement to commit genocide; attempt to commit genocide; [and] complicity in genocide," as punishable offensives under the 1948 convention. [49]

As a result of its vague wording, most scholars are in consensus that its definition is deficient, but there is little consensus on how it should be modified. [50] The deficient nature of the UN's legal definition, is why much of genocide scholarship is first concerned with how genocide should be defined and bound conceptually. The five main issues that scholars have with the UN definition of genocide are as follows: 1. "National, ethnical, racial or religious" groups were not defined, and has led to various interpretations. 2. The inclusion of "bodily or mental harm" suggests that there needs not be any "mass killing," which is rare and hard to prosecute. 3. The UN's use of controversial and ambiguous language in its definition has made it unlikely that genocides are declared as such. 4. The UN's definition excludes political groups and their motivations as possible perpetrators of genocide. And finally, 5. Their definition makes vague obligations to take action and does not spell out exactly how perpetrators are to be punished. The UN only lists "contracting parties" as responsible for prevention and punishment of genocide, but does not explain who that is. For these reasons, in addition to the UN's legal definition, during this study I have

---

[49] United Nations Office on Genocide Prevention and the Responsibility to Protect, "Convention on the Prevention and Punishment of the Crime of Genocide" (the United Nations), accessed September 12, 2017, www.un.org/en/genocideprevention/genocide.html.
[50] Adam Jones, *Genocide: A Comprehensive Introduction* (New York: Routledge, 2006), 13–14.

understood and defined genocide as the attempt (successful or unsuccessful) of the dominant/ruling group to destroy another "recognized, stable, and permanent group" designated as inferior, by the perpetrator due to racial, ethnic, religious and/or political differences.[51] All of which aims to eliminate the social and cultural norms that bind members of the targeted community, and thus results in its dissolution.

The term "ethnic cleansing" first came into use by the popular international media in the 1990s at the beginning of the war in Bosnia (1992). In its original use, it referred to "the practices of mass killing, torture, rape and forcible confinement into labor camps."[52] Ethnic cleansing and genocide did not become distinct legal categorizations until the war crimes proceedings took place in The Hague. As a result of this ruling, scholars have debated whether ethnic cleansing is or is not separate from genocide. Scholars in favor of the term, like Andrew Bell-Fialkof and Norman M. Naimark, explain ethnic cleansing as "the expulsion of an 'undesirable' population from a given territory due to religious or ethnic discrimination, political, strategic or ideological considerations, or a combination of these."[53] The divergent point between the two sides is intentionality. Scholars in favor of the distinction claim that

---

[51] John M Cox, *To Kill a People: Genocide in The Twentieth Century*, 2017, 11.

[52] Veena Das, "Collective Violence and the Shifting Categories of Communal Riots, Ethnic Cleansing and Genocide.," in *The Historiography of Genocide*, ed. Dan Stone (New York, NY: Palgrave Macmillan, 2008), 117.

[53] Andrew Bell-Fialkoff, "A Brief History of Ethnic Cleansing," *Foreign Affairs* 72, no. 3 (1993): 110, https://doi.org/10.2307/20045626.

in genocide the intent of the perpetrators is to kill while the intent in cases of ethnic cleansing is to remove.[54]

Scholars who find issue with the term ethnic cleansing first label it as a "perpetrator's term," arguing that genocide "privileges the perspective of the victims and survivors."[55] Further, the established genocidal framework is inclusive of all crimes of mass atrocity, and it is under this that ethnic cleansing should be addressed. As the difference between both genocide and ethnic cleansing is minute scholars like Martin Shaw, have been quick to point out the flaws in defining ethnic cleansing as separate. Even scholars who argue for the distinction, such as Andrew Bel-Fialkoff, concede that "cleansing…defies easy definition," and Norman M. Naimark admits that "ethnic cleansing bleeds into genocide."[56] If this is the case, and the distinction between ethnic cleansing and genocide are near indistinguishable, then why make the distinction at all. Those arguing for ethnic cleansing posit that as the goal of ethnic cleansing is simply to remove it can be done peacefully, and as such is different than genocide. Further, these instances of ethnic cleansing have led genocide scholars to point out that peaceful ethnic cleansing/removal is historically improbable. The forced deportation/removal of Greeks in Turkey is an excellent example of this.

---

[54] Norman M. Naimark, *Fires of Hatred: Ethnic Cleansing in Twentieth-Century Europe* (Cambridge, MA: Harvard University Press, 2001), 3.

[55] Martin Shaw, *What Is Genocide?* (Cambridge: Polity, 2007), 159.

[56] Andrew Bell-Fialkoff, "A Brief History of Ethnic Cleansing," *Foreign Affairs* 72, no. 3 (1993): 110–21, https://doi.org/10.2307/20045626; Naimark, *Fires of Hatred: Ethnic Cleansing in Twentieth-Century Europe*, 3–4.

In the case of the Greeks, scholars like Mark Mazower and Erik Sjöberg have deemed ethnic cleansing as a more appropriate term than genocide. This is largely due to the fact that during the early stages of deportation and expulsion, there were few "outright massacres."[57] While this may be the case it is important to note the varying typologies of genocide such as cumulative and retributive genocide that are applicable to the case of the Greeks.[58] According to Tessa Hofmann the genocide that occurred in Turkey at this time was unique and "must be described as cumulative state crime" that was conducted in phases, and with subsequently changing "crime scenes" across East Thrace and Asia Minor over a period of almost ten years.[59] The "cumulative" nature posited by Hofmann points to the building nature of policies which began slowly with socio-political exclusion and dehumanization of Greeks and other minorities in the Ottoman Empire, building to "increased radicalization" of the Balkan Wars,

---

[57] George N. Shirinian, ed., *The Asia Minor Catastrophe and the Ottoman Greek Genocide: Essays on Asia Minor, Pontos, and Eastern Thrace, 1912-1923* (The Asia Minor and Pontos Hellenic Research Center Inc., 2012), 39.

[58] Racho Donef, "The Role of Teşkilât-I Mahsua (Special Organization)," in *The Genocide of the Ottoman Greeks: Studies in State-Sponsored Campaign of Extermination of the Christians of Asia Minor, 1912-1922 and Its Aftermath: History, Law, Memory* (Aristide D. Caratzas, 2011), 179–94; Faltaits, *The Genocide of the Greeks in Turkey*. Genocide typologies are modified definitions of genocide which conceptually bind and defend unique instances/types of genocide.

[59] Tessa Hofmann, "Γενοκτονία Εν Ροή: Cumulative Genocide The Massacres and Deportations of the Greek Population of the Ottoman Empire (1912-1923)," in *The Genocide of the Ottoman Greeks: Studies in State-Sponsored Campaign of Extermination of the Christians of Asia Minor, 1912-1922 and Its Aftermath: History, Law, Memory* (Aristide D. Caratzas, 2011), 39–112; "Prologue," in *The Genocide of the Greeks in Turkey: Survivor Testimonies From The Nicomedia (Izmit) Massacres of 1920-1921* (River Vale, NJ, 2016).

and ultimately culminating in the "policies of violent persecution, deportations, large-scale massacres, and population exchange from 1914 onward."[60] Hoffman suggests that as a cumulative genocide, Turks needed time to build up the policies that began as discrimination and ended in genocide without interference from Greece. According to Hofmann, the building nature of a cumulative genocide allowed for this.[61]

Further, the cumulative nature of the Greek Genocide is shown in research by John Mourelos which discusses the first and failed attempt at population exchange between the Turks the Greeks in 1914. He explains how violence against Greeks in Asia Minor was able to occur for so long without international intervention. Mourelos goes on to conclude that the failure of the negotiations had been planned from the beginning by the Turks. These negotiations were simply a "smokescreen behind which to cover the" continued removal of the Ottoman Greeks through "obstructionist tactics of the Turkish representatives" during negotiations, in addition to

---

[60] Tessa Hofmann, Matthias Bjørnlund, and Vasileios Meichanetsidis, *The Genocide of the Ottoman Greeks: Studies on the State-Sponsored Campaign of Extermination of the Christians of Asia Minor (1912-1922) and Its Aftermath: History, Law, Memory* (New York: Aristide D. Caratzas, 2011), 14.

[61] Tessa Hofmann, "Γενοκτονία Εν Ροή: Cumulative Genocide The Massacres and Deportations of the Greek Population of the Ottoman Empire (1912-1923)," in *The Genocide of the Ottoman Greeks: Studies in State-Sponsored Campaign of Extermination of the Christians of Asia Minor, 1912-1922 and Its Aftermath: History, Law, Memory* (Aristide D. Caratzas, 2011), 39–112.

the continued persecutions with "unabated impetus" against Greeks at the time.[62]

The second typology, retributive genocide, originally coined by Vahakn N. Dadrian, is defined as "localized atrocities [used] as a form of meting out punishment to a segment of the minority, challenging or threatening the dominant group."[63] Helen Fein elaborates on Dadrian's explanation stating that cases of retributive genocide include cases "in which an elite of a dominant ethnic group destroys a significant part of another group which it fears will take its place as the dominant group."[64] The danger of this categorization of genocide is that it can be used to justify the violent actions of the perpetrators. Hofmann, Bjørnlund, and Meichanetsidis explain that within genocide studies, some scholars believe that the only *genuine* victims of genocide are those who are *innocent*.

The construct of innocence, when applied to ethno-religious minority groups, can only be maintained by exhibiting loyalty to those in power "under all circumstances and [innocent victims must] abstain from any irredentist or separatist sentiments, movements, or violent actions, including even cases of self-defense."[65] Hofmann, Bjørnlund, and Meichanetsidis explain the dangerous misconceptions that can occur if "the idea of

---

John Mourelos, "The 1914 Persecutions of Greeks in the Ottoman Empire and the First Attempt at an Exchange of Minorities between Greece and Turkey," in Hofmann, Bjørnlund, and Meichanetsidis, 113–36.

[63] Vahakn N Dadrian, "A Typology of Genocide," *Intrevmodsoc International Review of Modern Sociology* 5, no. 2 (1975): 201–12.

[64] Helen Fein, "Genocide and Other State Murders in the Twentieth Century" (United States Holocaust Memorial Museum, October 24, 1995).

[65] Hofmann, Bjørnlund, and Meichanetsidis, *The Genocide of the Ottoman Greeks*, 4–5.

genocide as reaction to provocative acts…the so-called provocation thesis" or retributive genocide is applied to the perpetrators of genocide. They firmly state that retributive justifications of genocide can never be applied to the perpetrators because;

> massacres, death marches, compulsory labor under conditions that make survival of the laborers virtually impossible cannot be held against the victim groups real or alleged political "disloyalty," their aspirations for autonomy or even separatism, or their attempted armed resistance against genocidal methods.[66]

Therefore, despite the fact that the acts of the Greek minority against their Turkish perpetrators *could* be explained and justified as retributive genocide; to do so would justify the Turkish Republic's state sponsored denial and their continued refusal to take responsibility for the crimes committed against Christian minorities.

Despite these methods of categorization, the plight of the Greeks and the Assyrians is not as widely accepted as that of the Armenians. Scholars attribute this to: 1. Availability of documentation and research in western languages, of which there is much on the Armenian genocide; 2. The international push for recognition of the Armenian case has existed for decades, while movements of the Greeks and Assyrians are more recent and smaller; 3. The official narrative of the Turkish government attributes

---

[66] Hofmann, Bjørnlund, and Meichanetsidis, *The Genocide of the Ottoman Greeks*, 8–9.

any loss of life in the name of "self-defense during civil insurrection and wartime," and as such the actions which occurred cannot be called genocide; 4. Some suggest that as a treaty between the Greek and Turkish government was signed in 1922 agreeing to a population exchange, this somehow proves that Turkey had no genocidal intent against its Greek citizens, and further that if there was any mismanagement then the Greek government was just as responsible as the Turkish. At this juncture it is important to note that the argument that there was a "mutually signed agreement" assenting to the population exchange between Greece and Turkey ignores the fact that the government in Ankara declared their intent to remove all Greeks from Turkish soil—prior to a legitimate agreement (Lausanne 1922) or method of exchange/removal was ever discussed.[67]

As stated previously, the distinguishing factor between cleansing and genocide lies with proving intent, which can be exceedingly difficult by judicial standards. For scholars not convinced by Hofmann's definition of cumulative genocide, one only need look at Articles 2 and 3 of the UN Convention to see that the Armenian, Greek and Assyrian victims in Turkey, meet all listed criterion.[68] George N. Shirinian, poignantly points out that as genocide is both a scholarly and legal concept, and to "restrict historical enquiry to legal rules of evidence" would

---

[67] George N. Shirinian, *The Asia Minor Catastrophe and the Ottoman Greek Genocide: Essays on Asia Minor, Pontos, and Eastern Thrace, 1912-1923*, 37.
[68] Articles II and III of the UN Convention on Genocide are listed and discussed in the section prior to this.

"impede historical justice."[69] As such, it is the responsibility of scholars to acknowledge and research all instances of genocide which include the Greeks in Turkey.

Jargon aside, both terms aim to define specific crimes against humanity in an effort to prosecute the governments and people responsible for the atrocities. Legally, for an individual or state to be tried and convicted of the crime of genocide, prosecutors must prove "intentionality." Veena Das points out that in cases of crimes against humanity, including ethnic cleansing, even with an overwhelming amount of evidence—one of two results is likely: 1. The large scale of the event leaves only a few people responsible and convicted; 2. There is a shift from punishment to reconciliation.[70] Whether ethnic cleansing is wholly different, similar, or synonymous to genocide is up to the individual scholar to decide.

Though it is important to consider the moral and educational implications that are associated with the study of genocide. Lemkin said it best, as his studies continued the numbers of victims across history continued to multiply. It was then that he understood that "the function of memory is not only to register past events, but to stimulate human conscience...[nations] must understand that an attack on one of them is an attack on all of them."[71] Thus, the "excessive exclusivity" used in the application of

---

[69] George N. Shirinian, 39–40.
[70] Das, "Collective Violence and the Shifting Categories of Communal Riots, Ethnic Cleansing and Genocide.," 118.
The wars in reference being World War I, the Balkan Wars, the Greek-Turkish War
[71] Raphael Lemkin quoted in George N. Shirinian, *The Asia Minor Catastrophe and the Ottoman Greek Genocide,* 40-41.

the term genocide because of fear of political/international backlash, hinders our ability to fully analyze the history of humanity.[72] The importance of community and collective memory will be discussed further in Chapter III, but it is important to note here that validation of memory is an important aspect of community building on a national and international scale.

Aside from works debating genocide versus ethnic cleansing, in the last ten years there has been an effort to broaden scholarship pertaining to the Greek Genocide in order to bring attention to this largely unknown historical event. Examples of this are organizations like the Pontian Greek Society of Chicago (PGSC) and the Pan Pontian Federation of the USA and Canada (PPFUC). Together they have held scholarly conferences to promote the study of and discussion about the Hellenic experience in Asia Minor, Pontus, and Eastern Thrace from the early-twentieth century and after the "Great Catastrophe" of 1912-1913.[73] Leading scholars who presented at these conferences such as Tessa Hofmann, Matthias Bjørnlund, and Harry J. Psomiades, have continued to publish in this field in an attempt to broaden the scholarship available to students and

---

[72] George N. Shirinian, *The Asia Minor Catastrophe and the Ottoman Greek Genocide*, 41.

[73] George N. Shirinian, 9.
Both academic conferences in question were held in Rosemont, IL on November 7, 2009 and was entitled "Academic Conference on the Asia Minor Catastrophe," while the November 6, 2010 conference was called "The Third Academic Conference on the Pontian and Anatolian Greek Genocide."George N. Shirinian, *The Asia Minor Catastrophe and the Ottoman Greek Genocide: Essays on Asia Minor, Pontos, and Eastern Thrace, 1912-1923*, 9.George N. Shirinian, 9.

professionals alike.[74] The efforts of these genocide scholars paid off in 2011 and 2012 when two separate edited collections dedicated exclusively to the Genocide of the Greeks were published.

The First, *The Genocide of the Ottoman Greeks: Studies on the State-Sponsored Campaign of Extermination of the Christians of Asia Minor (1912-1922) and Its Aftermath: History, Law, Memory,* edited by Hofmann, Bjørnlund, and Vasileios Meichanetsidis looks largely at why and how the Greek Genocide took place with less focus on the experience of the victims themselves.[75] Scholars also discussed the conditions that Greeks were forced to endure during their forced removal, and even the impact of international aid organizations on their survival—though little is dedicated to the perspective of the Greeks.[76] The perspective of survivors is more present in the essays that focus on how to teach, remember, and interpret genocide based on available scholarship in addition to surviving photographs and memorials that are erected by survivors across refugee communities in Greece.[77]

---

[74] Hofmann, Bjørnlund, and Meichanetsidis, *The Genocide of the Ottoman Greeks.*

[75] John Mourelos, "The 1914 Persecutions of Greeks in the Ottoman Empire and the First Attempt at an Exchange of Minorities between Greece and Turkey," in Hofmann, Bjørnlund, and Meichanetsidis, 113–36.

[76] Stavros T. Stavridis, "International Red Cross: A Mission to Nowhere," in Hofmann, Bjørnlund, and Meichanetsidis, 277–98; Harry J. Psomiades, "The American Near East Relief (NER) and the Megale Katastrophe in 1922," in Hofmann, Bjørnlund, and Meichanetsidis, 245–64.

[77] Ronald Levitsky, "Teaching the Greek Genocide," in Hofmann, Bjørnlund, and Meichanetsidis, 341–50; Michel Bruneau and Kyriakos Papoulidis, "Remembering the Genocide of the 'Unforgettable Homelands:' The Erection of Commemorative Monuments in Greece by the Refugees of Asia Minor," in Hofmann, Bjørnlund, and

The second collection, edited by George N. Shirinian, *The Asia Minor Catastrophe and the Ottoman Greek Genocide: Essays on Asia Minor, Pontos and Eastern Thrace, 1912-1923,* was published by the Asia Minor and Pontos Hellenic Research Center (AMPHRC), and is a product of the 2009 and 2010 conferences held by the PGSC and the PPFUC.[78] This collection of essays has works from many leading scholars in the field such as Tessa Hofmann, Matthias Bjørnlund, Harry J. Psomiades, and Armenian Genocide Scholar Tanner Akçam. The articles in the book offer similar studies to that of *The Genocide of the Greeks*. The collection edited by Shirinian gives a political, social and historical background while also discussing a broad variety of topics including Turkish violations of international law, the Smyrna Catastrophe, lack of recognition internationally, as well as a discussion of refugee identity and memory in Greece.[79] Notably

---

Meichanetsidis, 351–70; Abraham Der Krikorian and Eugene Taylor, "Achieving Ever-Greater Precision in Attestation and Attribution of Genocide Photogrpahs," in Hofmann, Bjørnlund, and Meichanetsidis, 389–434.

[78] George N. Shirinian, *The Asia Minor Catstrophe and the Ottoman Greek Genocide: Essays on Asia Minor, Pontos, and Eastern Thrace, 1912-1923* (Bloomingdale: The Asia Minor and Pontos Hellenic Research Center INC, 2012).

[79] Van Coufoudakis, "From Lausanne (1923) to Cyprus (2009): Turkey's Violations of International Law and the Destruction of Historic Hellenic Communities," in *The Asia Minor Catastrophe and the Ottoman Greek Genocide: Essays on Asia Minor, Pontos, and Eastern Thrace, 1912-1913,* ed. George N. Shirinian (Bloomingdale: The Asia Minor and Pontos Research Center INC, 2012), 249-272; Matthias Bjørnlund, "The Persecution of Greeks and Armenians in Smyrna, 1914-1916: A Special Case in the Course of the Late Ottoman Genocides," in *The Asia Minor Catastrophe and the Ottoman Greek Genocide,* ed. George N. Shirinian (Bloomingdale: The Asia Minor and Pontos Research Center INC, 2012), 89-134; Constantine Hatzidimitriou, "The Destruction of Smyrna in 1922: American Sources and Turkish Responsibility," in *The Asia Minor Catastrophe and the Ottoman Greek Genocide,* ed. George N. Shirinian (Bloomingdale: The Asia Minor and Pontos Research Center INC, 2012), 155-28; Robert J. Pranger, "U.S. Policy

Akçam's article discusses anti-Greek measures of the Young Turks pre-World War I as a prelude to the Armenian deportations that took place shortly after.[80] In this particular article Akçam does not use the term genocide a single time in reference to either the Greeks or the Armenians, due to the fact that terms like ethnic cleansing or massacre are "less problematic term[s]" than genocide.[81] Despite these two books being the only edited collections that specifically addressed the plight of the Greeks they managed to cover a wide range of subjects, and to lend weight the argument that continues to rage about the legitimacy of the claim of genocide.

Helping in this claim, are a limited number of published and translated collections of witness and survivor accounts. Harry Tsirikinidis' *At Last We Uprooted Them,* publishes a variety of translated documents from the French archives pertaining specifically to Greeks in Pontos and Asia Minor. Most significantly, is *The Genocide of the Greeks in Turkey: Survivor Testimonies from the Nicomedia (Izmit) Massacres of 1920-1921* by Kostas

in Recognizing the Genocides of Christian Minorities in the Late Ottoman Empire: Challenges and Opportunities," in *The Asia Minor Catastrophe and the Ottoman Greek Genocide,* ed. George N. Shirinian (Bloomingdale: The Asia Minor and Pontos Research Center INC, 2012), 273-290; Alexander Kitroeff, "Asia Minor Refugees in Greece: A History of Identity and Memory, 1920s-1980s," in *The Asia Minor Catastrophe and the Ottoman Greek Genocide,* ed. George N. Shirinian (Bloomingdale: The Asia Minor and Pontos Research Center INC, 2012), 229-248.

[80] Tanner Akçam, "The Greek Deportations and Massacres of 1913-1914: A Trial Run for the Armenian Genocide," in *The Asia Minor Catastrophe and the Ottoman Greek Genocide,* ed. George N. Shirinian (Bloomingdale: The Asia Minor and Pontos Research Center INC, 2012), 69-88.

[81] Tanner Akçam, *Young Turks' Crime* (2012): 55, 97 quoted in Erik Sjöberg, *The Making of the Greek Genocide* (New York: Berghahn, 2017), 36.

Faltaits. This primary source offers interviews with
survivors of the genocide while still in the process of
removal, and as such, offers unparalleled insight into their
experiences.[82] *The Genocide of the Greeks in Turkey*, was
originally titled *These are the Turks* and released in 1921.
Faltaits wrote this book in retaliation to a review by the
Inter-Allied Commission of Inquiry in May 1921 which
was sent by Allied forces to assess claims of atrocities on
behalf of both the Greeks and the Turks. Faltaits felt so
strongly that the Commission's report was incomplete and
biased that he took it upon himself to record the stories of
survivors that he encountered in Nicomedia in order to
more accurately portray who the Turks were, and the
atrocities that they were responsible for. The testimonies he
recorded occurred within the Nicomedia Region of Asia
Minor and/or were recounted to him there by refugees who
fled there. Nicomedia was comprised of eighteen
predominantly Greek villages and was surrounded by a
large number of Turkish villages. This region is bordered
by the Black Sea to the north, The Propontis (Sea of
Marmara) and the Gulf of Nicomedia (Gulf of Izmit) to the
west and the Sangarius River (Sakarya River) to the South,
with the easternmost village being Karapelit.[83]

Aside from edited collections, there are few
scholarly monographs that specifically concern the plight
of either the Anatolian or Pontian Greeks. Renée

[82] Kostas Faltaits, *The Genocide of the Greeks in Turkey: Survivor Testimonies From The Nicomedia (Izmit) Massacres of 1920-1921*, ed. Ellene Phoufas-Jousma and Aris Tsilfidis (River Vale, NJ, 2016).
[83] Faltaits, *The Genocide of the Greeks in Turkey: Survivor Testimonies From The Nicomedia (Izmit) Massacres of 1920-1921*.

Hirschon's *Heirs of the Greek Catastrophe: The Social Life of Asia Minor Refugees in Piraeus*, is one such volume. Hirschon takes an in-depth ethnographic look at the social lives of the refugees who settled in Kokkinia, near Piraeus beginning in 1923. Hirschon endeavors to find out how/if the refugees assimilated into the communities around them while still maintaining their own unique identity. This book discusses the plight and process of removal of the Greeks from Turkey, in passing at best. Beginning her survey of events with the Treaty of Sèvres (1920) the author focuses less on the violence leading up to and after the culminating events Smyrna. By choosing to not label the events that led to the displacement of the refugees in Kokkinia as neither genocide nor ethnic cleansing, it clear that her focus was on the lives of refugees post-removal and nothing else.[84]

Though there are few scholarly works, there are an ample number of monographs published by descendants of survivors and other professionals. The majority of these focus almost exclusively on the culminating events at Smyrna, as this is where the majority of English language primary sources come from.[85] Worth noting, are books like *Not Even My Name,* by Thea Halo, and *The Holocaust of the Pontian Greeks,* by Theodora Ioannidou. Halo takes the account of her mother and transposes it into a captivating

---

[84] Renée Hirschon, *Heirs of the Greek Catastrophe: The Social Life of Asia Minor Refugees in Piraeus* (Oxford: Berghahn Books, 1998).

[85] Majorie Housepian Dobkin, *Smyrna 1922: The Destruction of a City*, 4th edition (New York, NY: Newmark Press, 1998); Christos Papoutsky, *Ships of Mercy: The True Story of the Rescue of the Greeks, Smyrna, September 1922* (Portsmouth, N.H: Peter Randall Pub, 2008); Lydia Karagianis, *Smoldering Smyrna* (New York: Carlton Pr, 1996); Lou Urenekc, *Smyrna, September 1922: The American Mission to Rescue Victims of the 20th Century's First Genocide* (New York: Harper Collins, 2015)

narrative story that describes her peaceful and happy life in Anatolia, the devastation that followed upon forced removal, and her life in the United States. Ioannidou translates the accounts of eleven Pontic survivors' testimony from the original Pontic dialect into English narrative. While not strictly scholarly, these two books make an important contribution to the field by detailing the lives of Greeks in Anatolia at the time and discussing the tragedies they both witnessed and were a part of.

Since the passing of the International Association of Genocide Scholar's 2007 Resolution, scholars studying the Greek Genocide have begun the arduous process of attempting to understand why it has been largely ignored by their peers in the larger historiography of genocide. Israel Charny, member and former president of the International Association of Genocide Scholars, points out that in many cases victim groups within genocides who often suffered alongside each other are loathe to acknowledge that any group other than themselves suffered, or they do not want them explained as the same event. He further explains that in 2007 when the IAGS convened to pass the resolution acknowledging the Pontic Greeks, Anatolian Greeks, and Assyrians alongside Armenians—scholars that had studied and included the Greek element of the Armenian genocide in their studies—objected to the resolution and delayed its passing for months.[86]

---

[86]Israel W. Charny, "The Integrity and Courage to Recognize All the Victims of Genocide," in Hofmann, Bjørnlund, and Meichanetsidis, 21–38; Michel Bruneau and Kyriakos Papoulidis, "Remembering the Genocide of the 'Unforgettable Homelands:'

As mentioned previously, the plight of the Greeks ranges from being mentioned in passing, ignored completely and/or is outright denied. The official Turkish version of historiography continues to deny the occurrence of genocide, Greek, Armenian or otherwise completely. Their deportations are generally qualified as having been a necessary action to mitigate the threat of minority groups that had a history of "disloyalty" to the government. By resettling them out of combat zones and into other areas, the minority groups in question would cease to threaten national security.[87] Turkish denial generally manifests in one of two ways (sometimes both): 1. to find "scapegoats" for "security measures gone awry," saying "unscrupulous officials, Kurds, and common criminals" were at fault. 2. When accused, the Turkish government responds "with silence, diplomatic efforts, and political pressure" when possible to maintain their position of innocence.[88]

In *The Balkans: A Short History,* and *Salonica: City of Ghosts Christians, Muslims and Jews 1430-1950,* Mark Mazower understates the extent of the atrocity committed by the Turks in their efforts to create a homogenous

---

The Erection of Commemorative Monuments in Greece by the Refugees of Asia Minor," in Hofmann, Bjørnlund, and Meichanetsidis, 351–70.

[87] Erik Sjöberg, *The Making of the Greek Genocide: Contested Memories of the Ottoman Greek Catastrophe* (New York: Berghahn Books, 2017), 32. While I have many reservations about a number of the conclusions drawn from Sjöberg's work, explained later on, his research of historic events and summaries of the various fields and groups he seeks to analyze I have found well researched and succinct.

[88] Roger Smith, Eric Markusen, and Robert Jay Lifton, "Professional Ethics and the Denial of Armenian Genocide," *Holocaust and Genocide Studies* 9, no. 1 (1995): 1–22.

Turkey.[89] In both works the word genocide is never used,
favoring instead ethnic cleansing to describe the violence
that occurred at the time. Only the Armenian minority is
mentioned in passing, and only once in reference to the
violence they were subject to. *The Balkans,* was published
in 2000, and so the exclusion of the Greek genocide can be
explained as it had not yet been internationally recognized,
but the Armenian genocide was officially recognized by
IAGS in 1997. As such, its exclusion from Mazower's
narrative seems out of place. I find it perplexing that
Mazower spends the majority of his writing justifying the
various rebellions and declarations of independence all
over the Balkans and within the Ottoman Empire, but fails
to acknowledge the extent of the violence perpetrated
against Christian minority groups by the government they
were rebelling against.[90] Further, in *Salonika,* Mazower
explains the population exchange between Greece and
Turkey as a legitimate legal exchange as agreed upon by
Elfteherios Venizelos and Mustafa Kemal Ataturk, ignoring
that the genocide was well underway before this, and that
the agreement was a result of the influx of refugees that had
been occurring.[91]

    Mazower is not unique in this point of view. As
mentioned previously, some scholars prefer to discuss the
plight of the Greeks in the context of ethnic cleansing

[89] Mark Mazower, *The Balkans: A Short History* (New York: The Modern Library,
2000); Mark Mazower, *Salonica, City of Ghosts: Christians, Muslims, and Jews, 1430-
1950* (New York: Vintage, 2006).
[90] Mark Mazower, *The Balkans: A Short History* (New York: The Modern Library,
2000).
[91] Mazower, *Salonica, City of Ghosts.*

rather than genocide.[92] Though most commonly scholars include Greeks as a minority group that suffered during the Armenian genocide, and thus imply that though some Greeks were killed by Turkey they were not singled out as the Armenians were.[93] The most recent example of this comes from Erik Sjöberg's *The Making of the Greek Genocide: Contested Memories of the Ottoman Greek Catastrophe.* Though Sjöberg claims that the purpose of his work is not to determine if "the violence against the Ottoman Greeks was genocidal or not," his choice of language as well as the framing of his argument make it clear that the "notion of the Greek Genocide" exists only in the "national imagination of the Greeks" that has undergone a "redefinition of national experience" in recent years.[94] Despite this, Sjöberg offers an in-depth discussion of the politics surrounding the Greek Genocide and of the arguments both for and against this designation. While he never outright denies that the crimes against the Greeks at the time constituted genocide, he continuously points to prominent Armenian scholars, like Taner Akçam, who prefer the designation of ethnic cleansing. Sjöberg proffers that ultimately, legal designation as genocide or not is unimportant. What is important is that of moral culpability. Simply, the admission that a criminal act occurred is necessary in order for the cycle of action that allows for any national security concern to be met with violence or the

---

[92] Norman M. Naimark, *Fires of Hatred: Ethnic Cleansing in Twentieth-Century Europe* (Cambridge, MA: Harvard University Press, 2001).

[93] John M Cox, *To Kill a People: Genocide in The Twentieth Century*, 2017; Adam Jones, *Genocide: A Comprehensive Introduction* (New York: Routledge, 2006).

[94] Sjöberg, *The Making of the Greek Genocide*, 1–8.

restriction of civil liberties.[95] While this may be true, it does not negate the importance of labeling genocidal events as such. Nor does it negate the importance convicting and prosecuting those responsible for genocidal crimes. Both of which are important in discouraging and preventing future genocide from occurring in that they set the precedent that such actions will not be tolerated and are punishable under international law.

Genocide denial is considered by many scholars to be the last phase of genocide, and can come in a variety of forms. Perpetrators can claim their actions were merely in self-defense, that the deaths/violence in question were not intentional or that the violence was mutual and justified.[96] The motivation behind this can be for "self-serving ideology, bigotry, intellectual confusion, careerism, identification with power...[or] a particular conception of knowledge."[97] Some scholars exploit the ambiguity of the UN Genocide Convention using it as a black and white guideline to define what is or is not genocide. It begs the question if there can ever truly be a method of measurement, whether legal or historical, that can definitively and with no questions pass judgement.

Sjöberg credits a "shift in historical writing" that gives weight to witness testimonies of civilians rather than documents/accounts exclusively from heads of state, politicians or soldiers, and as a result has given nations the

---

[95] Sjöberg, 236.
[96] Jones, *Genocide: A Comprehensive Introduction*, 352–53.
[97] Smith, Markusen, and Lifton, "Professional Ethics and the Denial of Armenian Genocide," 14.

ability to *reimagine* their story of the past.[98] This point of view suggests by adding witness testimonies into the larger historical narrative, and because it challenges state-sponsored historiographies, they are somehow invalid. Witness testimonies or the perspective of civilians are equally important to accounts of those in power. To exclude either form of evidence would result in an incomplete understanding of the past, and to deem one as more or less reliable than the other is irresponsible.

Some scholars put less weight in the testimonies of witnesses because people's memories change and they may over/under-state what occurred, but in general just as memories can be warped over time, so can the documents that inform histories. Documents can and have been proven false. Bias exists in all accounts of history and in all forms of historic evidence, and it is the responsibility of scholars to extrapolate fact based on all available evidence. This is why the account of victims, interviewed in 1920-1921 by Kostas Faltaits during the process of removal from Nicomedia, which as of 2016 was made available in English, is so important and will be the primary source base of this study.[99]

Genocide results in the loss of human life, communities, and culture. The ethnic-Greeks in Turkey, are largely overlooked by scholars as legitimate victims of genocide. Instead, they favor more readily researchable topics offering a wider source base available in English,

[98] Sjöberg, *The Making of the Greek Genocide: Contested Memories of the Ottoman Greek Catastrophe*, 223.
[99] Faltaits, *The Genocide of the Greeks in Turkey*.

and which boast scores of scholarly research to build on. Because of the dearth source base, the Greek Genocide can and should be studied within the context of the larger Christian genocide that occurred in Turkey until more sources are available.

Overall, the scholarship pertaining to the Greek Genocide is narrow, and is restricted by the debates that continue in its definition as a genocide and available source material. Available primary sources have come largely from either the Western European countries or from the United States and limit the arguments that can be made, and is lacking in first-hand accounts of survivors. It is here that this study seeks to step in. In the second chapter by utilizing a primary source base that is comprised of interviews from survivors on their way out of Turkey, this analysis is able to show the extent of Turkish violence against the Greeks at the time. Additionally, some scholarly articles look at the memory of the genocide in Greece and at the lives of refugees in Greece, but not elsewhere. It is for this reason, that in chapter three I look at the institutions and social groups in the United States that strive to preserve the heritage and memory of their ancestors. Therefore, by utilizing the primary source testimonies documented by Kostas Faltaits I will first discuss how the Turks attempted to dismantle Greek communities in Asia Minor via genocidal violence in an effort to destroy the Greek's community ties and sense of identity to force them out of Turkey. Then, I will show how Greeks have preserved their unique culture and identity in the United States.

CHAPTER II

PATH TO GENOCIDE

Introduction:

The relationship between the Greeks and the Turks has been long and complex. Their rivalry arguably began after the fall of the Byzantine Empire and the subsequent conquest of their former territories by the rising Ottoman Empire. After the loss of territory the Greeks espoused their "μεγάλη ιδέα" (meh-gal-ee ee-day-a), or big idea, through which nationalists called for reclamation of lands from the Turks. While regional borders changed, the populations within did not. The ethnic-Greeks that lived in now Ottoman territory remained where they were despite changing borders. The Ottoman government and its millet system allowed the Greeks, or *rum* millet, to flourish within the Ottoman economy despite their "separate but inferior" status.[100] Through this ruling style, ethnic-Greeks were able to maintain their distinct cultural identity despite many no longer using the Greek language. For most their only connection to the physical country of Greece was their heritage and their religion, Greek Orthodox Christianity.[101] In order to better understand how the heterogeneous Ottoman Empire transformed into Mustafa Kemal's more homogeneous Turkish Republic in the mid-twentieth

---

[100] George N. Shirinian, ed., *The Asia Minor Catastrophe and the Ottoman Greek Genocide: Essays on Asia Minor, Pontos, and Eastern Thrace, 1912-1923* (The Asia Minor and Pontos Hellenic Research Center Inc., 2012), 12.
[101] Helen Papanikolas, *An Amulet of Greek Earth: Generations of Immigrant Folk Culture* (Athens: Swallow Press ; Ohio University Press, 2002).

century, we must first endeavor to understand the rise and role of nationalism in the Balkans and how it impacted both Greece and the Ottoman Empire.

Contextualizing Genocide:
Nationalism and Nation-Building in the Balkans:

As discussed in Chapter 1, scholars of modernist nationalism point to the French Revolution as the jumping off point for the nationalism that spread through Europe and created the modern nation-states that exist today. Modernist theory also explains that nation states are created only when nationalism in conjunction with industrialization or modernization of a society occurs. While this two part theory can be widely applied across Western European nations, it is not a perfect fit in the case of the Balkan states. In the Balkan states nationalism emerged from approximately 1804-1830, before there was any sign of industrialization in the region.[102] If we consider applying the conquest thesis, which points to violence and war making as a way for states to centralize and build power, we see that because of the "low organizational basis" and poor infrastructure "state building and warfare were fairly limited" in much of the nineteenth century Balkans.[103]

Even once Balkan nations gained their political independence, economic development/industrial growth was not guaranteed. With no national banks in any Balkan state until the mid-nineteenth century, and no "proper

---

[102] Malešević, "Did Wars Make Nation-States in the Balkans?: Nationalisms, Wars and States in the 19th and Early 20th Century South East Europe," 307; Mark Mazower, *The Balkans: A Short History* (New York: The Modern Library, 2000), 14, 43.

[103] Malešević, "Did Wars Make Nation-States in the Balkans?: Nationalisms, Wars and States in the 19th and Early 20th Century South East Europe," 308-309.

industrial base," exports from the region were dreadful.[104] The underdevelopment of these new nations is also evident in their lack of professional armies—for example the Greek and Serbian wars of independence were fought by bandits, "foreign trained volunteers…and local notables."[105] By the end of the nineteenth and beginning of the twentieth century the "small wars and weak [Balkan] states" that previously existed were radically transformed by "accelerated modernization and state building on the Western European model" and resulted in the "large scale protracted and highly destructive warfare" showcased in the First and Second Balkan Wars (1912-1913; 1913).[106]

Unlike Western European where states' prolonged warfare has been linked to successful long term state building, this was not the case in the Balkan states that remained infrastructurally weak—regardless of their winning/losing status post-Balkan Wars. Which can be attributed to the weakness of nationalism in this part of the world at the time.[107]Some historians argue that the Balkans were a "breeding ground of nationality" and that with the fall of both the Ottoman and Hapsburg Empires there was an "awakening of nationalities." Others disagree and argue that nationalism was politically irrelevant in the Balkans for most of the nineteenth century due to a lack of a "cross class ideology" that advocated for a unified culture, and thus demanded living in a politically independent sovereign

---

[104] Malešević, 309.
[105] Malešević, 309.
[106] Malešević, 311.
[107] Malešević, 313–14.

state.[108] It seems more likely that the latter is true, at least for the early part of the nineteenth century. Unlike the Western European states that emerged on the basis of "ancient national aspirations" and as a by-product of "strong national movements," the "new political entities" that emerged in the Balkan region were an "unintended" byproduct of the declining Ottoman Empire.[109]

These new Balkan states were subsequently run by rulers who attempted to gain power through an expanding "administrative strata" putting them in direct conflict with the much larger peasants classes. Conflicts over land between the "large scale peasantry and ever growing patrimonial bureaucrats" created highly polarized societies where most did not identify with their states.[110] Gellner points out that mass nationalism is impossible without "standardized languages, sate sponsored educational systems or high literacy rates" all of which were not present in the newly minted Balkan polities.[111] When nationalist rhetoric and ideology was finally disseminated and more widely accepted in the region, during the late-nineteenth and early-twentieth centuries, it was embraced by the small number of "military establishment, political and cultural elites and bureaucrats and their families."[112] In other words, those that were educated and exposed to western European

[108] Malešević, 315.
[109] Malešević, 325.
[110] Malešević, 325.
[111] Malešević, 325; Ernest Gellner, *Nations and Nationalism* (Oxford: Blackwell, 1983).
[112] Malešević, "Did Wars Make Nation-States in the Balkans?: Nationalisms, Wars and States in the 19th and Early 20th Century South East Europe," 325; John Agnew, "No Borders, No Nations: Making Greece in MAcedonia," *Annals of the Association of American Geographers* 97, no. 2 (June 2007): 404.

politics, theories and discourse—not the peasant majority who lived on the peripheries of these new nations.

As stated above, the new Balkan states were the product of slow spreading nationalist ideals from the west, the decline of the Ottoman Empire and protracted warfare in the late nineteenth and early twentieth centuries. The breaking up of empires into statelike units can also be seen as the result of "the spread of a model of territorial statehood and state-centered political economy from Western Europe."[113] This model of statehood is characterized by a strong center and the creation of immovable/unquestionable borders between the nation-state and their neighbors. In relation to nationalism, borders are considered to be constructed around particular national groups in an attempt to further homogenize the peoples within them by giving a specific identity as espoused by intellectuals and politicians.[114] Furthermore, as sovereign states exist only through the control of a specifically bounded area, and are legitimized by state sponsored histories tying them to the land, this creates "cultures [that] are thought of as naturally integral and territorial" to the nation-state.[115] "Historical rights" to territory are thus established and reinforced through nationalist ideologies that are spread through "media, school textbooks and lessons, and in everyday conversations" in order to firmly establish a "we" and a "they."[116] This was a common

---

[113] Agnew, "No Borders, No Nations: Making Greece in MAcedonia," 398.
[114] Agnew, 400–401.
[115] Agnew, 402.
[116] Agnew, 402–3.

practice that occurred in the bordering/establishment of what would become the Turkish Republic and modern Greece. To understand the impact of nationalist rhetoric and sharp immovable borders established, we must first understand how/why the Ottoman Empire transitioned from a heterogeneous empire with a policy of tolerance towards its non-Muslim minorities to a policy seeking homogeneity through Turkification.

Nationalism and the Ottoman Empire, the Young Turks and Mustafa Kemal

While imperfect in many ways, as a multi-ethnic empire, the Ottomans were relatively tolerant of the various minority groups over which they ruled. Through the millet system, each religious community was able to preside over their own affairs, operate with relative independence apart from the central government, use their own language, develop religious/educational/cultural institutions, and even collect taxes for the state. Still Muslim Turks considered members of minority groups as "separate and inferior," in comparison to themselves.[117]

In 1826 the Ottoman Empire began a radical process of modernization under the "infidel sultan" Mahmut II. First, he disbanded the Janissaries (imperial army) and proceeded to eliminate regional rivalries, curb religious class power, establish a French regimental military system and military schools. This period, the *Tanzimat* (reorganization) period, was officially brought into being with the Gülhane Rescipt (1839) and the Hatti Hümayun edict (1856). Both of these documents established "equality of citizenship before the law for Muslim and non-Muslim" alike, while maintaining the religious equality through the already established millet system.[118] Unfortunately, the policies of the Tanzimat

---

[117] George N. Shirinian, ed., *The Asia Minor Catastrophe and the Ottoman Greek Genocide: Essays on Asia Minor, Pontos, and Eastern Thrace, 1912-1923* (The Asia Minor and Pontos Hellenic Research Center Inc., 2012), 12.

[118] Virginia H. Aksan, "Ottoman to Turk: Continuity and Change," *International Journal* 61, no. 1 (Winter /2006 2005): 20–21.

proved to only exacerbate the animosity between Muslims and non-Muslims. The elite Muslim class, was increasingly impoverished despite holding prominent positions in the government and military; while the non-Muslim communities made up of Greeks, Armenians and Jews emerged as a wealthy commercial class. This first attempt at constitutionalism was short lived and ended when the Mehmet II was replaced with Sultan Abdulhamit II.[119]

While the Tanzimat period and the rule of Mehmet II were considered to have been modern and secular, Abdulhamit II's rule was decisively less so. Abdulhamit II suspended the constitution and sought to reinstate "the status and influence of the religious classes, and to reframe the empire as a Muslim caliphate."[120] During this period, the revolutionary Committee of Union and Progress (CUP or Young Turks) emerged among the officer class in Thessaloniki and gained momentum after the loss of Greece, Serbia, Bosnia and Bulgaria. Alarmed by the loss of territory and increasing European involvement led Muslims to call for "reform, constitutional liberties and imperial revival."[121] In an attempt to appease the CUP, Abdulhamit reinstated the constitution on July 23, 1908.[122] Despite this Abdulhamit was removed from power, exiled and replaced with his brother Reshad. Notwithstanding a counter-revolution in Constantinople perpetrated by those loyal to the sultan, the CUP was able to squelch the

---

[119] Aksan, 22–23.

[120] Aksan, 23.

[121] Mark Mazower, *Salonica, City of Ghosts: Christians, Muslims, and Jews, 1430-1950* (New York: Vintage, 2006), 255.

[122] Aksan, "Ottoman to Turk: Continuity and Change," 23.

"Hamidian sympathizers" who were subsequently replaced by "a more compliant government."[123] By 1909, with the sultan overthrown, the government was run by the CUP with the Three Pashas the helm—Enver, Cemal and Talat.[124]

The CUP originally sold itself as a having "values of cosmopolitan loyalty to the empire over the divisive power of nationalism," and stressed "common participation in a constitutional government" in the name of the people/the Ottoman nation.[125] This platform was widely supported by minorities who were interested in acquiring more rights under the constitution, and this was espoused during the CUP revolution. Despite this early platform after the Balkan Wars, and the loss of land to newer nation-states like Greece, the Young Turk politicians embarked on a "violent project of societal transformation" in order to guarantee the existence of a Turkish nation-state moving forward.[126]

Even before the onset of World War I the CUP "dreamt of building a strong, united society that was dominated by Ottoman Muslims."[127] The radical wing of the CUP, Turkish nationalists, believed that "coercion if not outright violence, could eventually help achieve their political vision for the future in ways that" diplomatic

---

[123] Mazower, *Salonica, City of Ghosts*, 259–60.

[124] Aksan, "Ottoman to Turk: Continuity and Change," 23.

[125] Mazower, *Salonica, City of Ghosts*, 261–62.

[126] Uğur Ümit Üngör, "Seeing like a Nation-State: Young Turk Social Engeineering in Eastern Turkey, 1913-50," *Journal of Genocide Research* 10, no. 1 (June 2008): 16.

[127] Üngör, 20.

negotiations would not.[128] As stated above, the Balkan
Wars served as a turning point that "traumatized" the
Young Turks while it simultaneously "polarized relations
among Ottoman political elites," which only further pushed
CUP leadership away from ideals of political pluralism
within their borders.[129] Additionally, the emergence of new
Balkan nation-states made up of former Ottoman subjects
that persecuted Ottoman Muslims only "confirmed
suspicions [with]in the CUP that non-Muslim and in
particular non-Turkish Ottomans could not be trusted" and
needed to be dealt with.[130]

As time moved forward, the pluralist Ottomanist
identity began to collapse and was replaced with the
various nationalist ideologies that spread largely among the
Christian minorities.[131] Similarly, ideas of Turkifikation
and Turkishness that had been discussed within the CUP
since it was first organized were popularized. But ideas of
Turkish nationalism began to gain momentum after CUP
party conferences were held in Salonica (1910,1911) and
Istanbul (1912, 1913). At these conferences CUP members
officially pushed for reform in two ways: national
education and national economy. The support of which
resulted in a process of "political polarization" that
intensified calls for "ethnic unmixing" within their

---

[128] Üngör, 20.
[129] Üngör, 20.
[130] Üngör, 20.
[131] Mazower, *Salonica, City of Ghosts*, 263.

borders."[132] It was during this period that the now infamous phrase, "Turkey for the Turks" emerged.

On January 23, 1913 the CUP officially seized power via coup with the intent of creating a nation-state from the remains of the Ottoman Empire. Despite the variety of languages, religions and cultures present, the CUP lead by Talat and Enver slowly began to introduce a campaign of Turkification across Ottoman society.[133] The two fold reform of national education and economy went into effect starting in 1914 when Muslim-Turks replaced non-Muslims in order to create a Turkish bourgeoise where Greeks and Armenians that dominated the commercial classes were replaced. By 1915 a language reform was passed which prohibited the use of any foreign languages other than Turkish in all economic transactions, in an effort to further promote Muslim-Turkish economic activity.[134]

The attempts to supplant Muslim-Turks into the commercial economy did not prove as successful as the CUP originally wanted, and so more "violent methods of Turkification of the economy" were employed— particularly along the Aegean littoral where most businesses were owned by Ottoman Greeks.[135] These more violent measures were executed by CUP emissaries such as Special Organization agents which causes an escalation

---

[132] Üngör, "Seeing like a Nation-State: Young Turk Social Engeineering in Eastern Turkey, 1913-50," 21.
[133] Erol Ülker, "Contextualizing 'Turkification': Nation-Building in the Late Ottoman Empire, 1908-18," *Nations and Nationalism* 11, no. 4 (2005): 622.
[134] Ülker, 622.
[135] Üngör, "Seeing like a Nation-State: Young Turk Social Engeineering in Eastern Turkey, 1913-50," 23.

from "boycotts and expropriations" to "kidnappings and assassinations of Greek business men and community leaders, and even whole sale deportation of villages."[136] By the summer of 1914 this "terror campaign" led many Ottoman Greeks to emigrate to Chios or Greece.

The final and arguably most important phase of Turkification were the "attempts at demographic and territorial nationalism" which sought to create a national Turkish core in Anatolia.[137] Turks claimed historical right to Anatolia, long before the rise of the CUP, and considered it the fatherland of all Turks. After the Balkan Wars and the loss of much of Macedonia, there was renewed focus on Anatolia as the "cradle of the empire and its Turkish stock."[138] Thus, the process of Turkifying Anatolia began first with boycotts against non-Muslims and eventually relying heavily on settlement and forced-migration policies. These more extreme policies were chosen in lieu of cultural assimilation because Greeks and Armenians were considered to have too "strong [of] national consciousnesses;" and as such could not ever be considered loyal Ottomans.[139]

After a successful population exchange of the Bulgarians in Thrace, the CUP looked to enact a similar policy with Greece in order to remove all Greeks living on the Aegean coast. A population exchange was first proposed by Turkey in May 1914, during which time the

---

[136] Üngör, 24.
[137] Ülker, "Contextualizing 'Turkification': Nation-Building in the Late Ottoman Empire, 1908-18," 622, 617.
[138] Ülker, 624.
[139] Ülker, 625.

government began a "systematic persecution" of Greeks in the area so as to expedite the acceptance of the proposal in Greece. At the time, the Turks denied the persecutions of Greeks in Anatolia, and by the time the Greek government consented the Ottoman Empire had entered WWI effectively ending negotiations.[140] The beginning of the war did not end persecutions, forced migrations or resettlements, they continued and a mass exodus of Christians from Anatolia began with WWI.

Prior to the outbreak of WWI in 1914, the Interior Minister Talaat ordered that all Greeks be cleansed from settlements on the coast, and replaced with Muslim refugees from the Balkans or from the interior or Turkey.[141] Later, in June 1915, according to German diplomatic correspondence, Talaat informed the German embassy of their intent to take "advantage of the World War in order to make a clean sweep of internal enemies—the indigenous Christians—without being hindered in doing so by diplomatic intervention from other countries."[142] The removal of the Greeks from Asia Minor was done in who ways. As early as July and August of 1914, adult males were conscripted into labor battalions or were forced to join

---

[140] John Mourelos, "The 1914 Persecutions of Greeks in the Ottoman Empire and the First Attempt at an Exchange of Minorities between Greece and Turkey," in *The Genocide of the Ottoman Greeks: Studies in State-Sponsored Campaign of Extermination of the Christians of Asia Minor, 1912-1922 and Its Aftermath: History, Law, Memory* (Aristide D. Caratzas, 2011), 113–36; Ülker, "Contextualizing 'Turkification': Nation-Building in the Late Ottoman Empire, 1908-18," 625.

[141] Tessa Hofmann, "The Genocide against the Christians in the Late Ottoman Period, 1912-1922," in *The Asia Minor Catastrophe,* ed. George N. Shirinian (New York: The Asia Minor and Pontos Hellenic Research Center INC, 2012), 49.

[142] Hofmann, "The Genocide Against," 50.

the *amele taburlari,* of the Ottoman army. Second, once the "intellectual elites of the Christian target groups had been destroyed," from 1915-1917 those remaining were deported.[143] Though the deportations in Nicomedia happened later, you will see that similar policies were employed. In the following sections, you will see that deportees were stripped of their personal belongings, separated from their family members, were frequently assaulted by members of *chettes,* and were routinely killed at will.[144]

In 1915, a year after the beginning of WWI, the CUP passed a law to "regulate the relocations of the groups that were considered potential traitors" which simply served as a means to justify the deportations that were already occurring.[145] The first group to be expelled were the Armenians and the Greeks followed, though the law in question did not specifically name them. The harsh measures used to "cleanse" Anatolia were not explicitly laid out by the government, but rather left up to the local leaders. Once these regions were cleared, Muslim immigrants that were brought in from other regions (including outside of the empire) and settled into villages previously occupied by non-Muslims. All of which was an effort to create a "Turkish national core" at the heart of its territory, Anatolia.

---

[143] Hofmann, "The Genocide Against," 51-52.

[144] Hofmann, "The Genocide Against," 52-53; Faltaits, *Genocide of the Greeks.*

[145] Ülker, "Contextualizing 'Turkification': Nation-Building in the Late Ottoman Empire, 1908-18," 626.

In 1918, the Ottoman Empire surrendered and the CUP dissolved itself—though it continued to operate under other names.[146] Following this and the end of WWI the Treaty of Sevres (1919) was signed between the Ottoman rump state and the Entente. Sevres was negotiated by Eleutherios Venizelos, the Prime Minister of Greece, which gave them control of the Turkish port city of Smyrna in order to protect the ethnic-Greeks in the area while simultaneously fulfilling irredentist nationalist goals to reincorporate Asia Minor into Greece. While this Greek occupation was sanctioned by the Allies, and agreed upon by the Sultan of the Ottoman Empire, both Greece and Turkey failed to ratify it into law. With assistance of former CUP leaders, Mustafa Kemal by sheer "force of personality and clever maneuvering, rallied Turks (Muslims) from all over Anatolia" to his Republican People's Party (RPP) and challenged the rump sultanate government in occupied Istanbul.[147] Under Mustafa Kemal, the RPP rejected this treaty and claimed that "the Anatolian Greeks on the Aegean and Pontic coasts supported the invading Hellenic Greek armies and their British sponsors," and as such needed to be removed from Turkey.[148] Believing that if allowed to remain the Greeks "would continue to serve as indigenous resources for enemies of the Turkish

---

[146] Aksan, "Ottoman to Turk: Continuity and Change," 24; Üngör, "Seeing like a Nation-State: Young Turk Social Engineering in Eastern Turkey, 1913-50," 28.
[147] Aksan, "Ottoman to Turk: Continuity and Change," 24; Üngör, "Seeing like a Nation-State: Young Turk Social Engineering in Eastern Turkey, 1913-50," 28.
[148] Norman M. Naimark, *Fires of Hatred: Ethnic Cleansing in Twentieth-Century Europe* (Cambridge, MA: Harvard University Press, 2001), 189.

republic."[149] The continued eastern advancement of the Greek Army in Asia Minor and persecutions of both Christian and Muslims in Asia minor ultimately led to the outbreak of the Greco-Turkish War in 1920.

The Turkish Republic was declared a nation-state in its own right on October 29, 1923, and with the end of Ottoman Empire also ended ideas of pan-Turkism and pan-Islamism. These ideals were instead replaced by the notion that a "Turk" was "a citizen of the new Turkish republic, regardless of his etho-religious identity."[150] The policies of national homogenization did not end with the dissolution of the CUP and rise of Kemal. Instead, Turkification was able to continue unabated and "untroubled by restraints of any kind" due to national sovereignty within their borders and international support for policies of modernization which included policies of social engineering, and would ultimately lead to continued genocidal violence.[151] It was during this period of Turkification that the Treaty of Lausanne was signed the Greek-Turkish convention of Lausanne on January 30, 1923. Here both Greece and Turkey agreed to a mutual and obligatory population exchange between countries. Ottoman Greek Christians would be sent to Greece, while Greek Muslims would be sent to Turkey. It is important to reiterate that this convention did not mark the beginning of forced removal or violence, both of which can be traced back to 1914.

---

[149] Naimark, 189.
[150] Üngör, "Seeing like a Nation-State: Young Turk Social Engineering in Eastern Turkey, 1913-50," 29; Aksan, "Ottoman to Turk: Continuity and Change," 25.
[151] Üngör, "Seeing like a Nation-State: Young Turk Social Engineering in Eastern Turkey, 1913-50," 29.

The ascent of Mustafa Kemal and the establishment of the Turkish Republic allowed Kemalists to draw clear borders around their nation-state and within which republican educational institutions were used to espouse and embrace Turkishness as evidenced by the expression "how happy is he who can say he is a Turk." This "educational authoritarianism" also shows the new country's narrative which eliminated the Ottoman past while "extolling the great Turkish history, the 10 great Turkish civilizations, and even [espoused] a sun language theory, which posited that all languages had their original source in the Turkic family."[152] By the time the 1925 Seyh Ssaid rebellion took place, Ataturk (Kemal) and Kemalists were able to oust the remaining religious leaders and unionist (Ottoman) sympathizers. It was at this point that they were able to create a Turkish state that was considered to be modern, secular and as not parallel to Islam. It is this contested legacy that persists today.[153]

---

[152] Aksan, "Ottoman to Turk: Continuity and Change," 25.
[153] Aksan, 25.

Nationalism and Greece:

While the Genocide of the Greeks took place in
Turkey, it is important to understand the role that
nationalism played in Greece in order to understand the
interstate relations that took place, and the sometimes
mutual violence that occurred. Greek nationalism began
with the creation of the *"Megale Idea" or* "Great Idea"
which first popularized by the revolutionary Regas
Velestinles in the late eighteenth century. It refers to an
irredentist concept that called for the "liberation and
unification of all areas predominately settled by ethnic
Greeks" into a unified nation-state made up of all former
territories in the Byzantine Empire, particularly the areas of
Asia Minor and Constantinople.[154]

Early Greek nationalists hoped to restore the glory
of ancient Greece by unifying all of the Greeks that were
scattered throughout the Balkan Peninsula, Macedonia,
Thrace and Asia Minor. The small Greek state that gained
independence in 1821 originally only had control of the
southern part of what constitutes the state today. In order to
achieve it irredentist goals Greek nationalists looked to use
a "fusion of ethnic and historical arguments to justify
territorial expansion" and to gain land from the rump of the
Ottoman Empire.[155] Greece was able to gain the support of
Western European powers in their bid to expand their

---

[154] Tessa Hofmann, Matthias Bjørnlund, and Vasileios Meichanetsidis, *The Genocide of the Ottoman Greeks: Studies on the State-Sponsored Campaign of Extermination of the Christians of Asia Minor (1912-1922) and Its Aftermath: History, Law, Memory* (New York: Aristide D. Caratzas, 2011), 444.

[155] Agnew, "No Borders, No Nations: Making Greece in Macedonia," 404.

borders because many "proclaimed ancient Athenian ideals, Hellenism 'created an idealized ancient Greece as the birthplace of European spirit and western civilization." As such, despite the fact that Greece had "fallen from its historic grace," with the help of European nations their "best values" could be revived once the "Ottoman yoke" was removed.[156]

In order to expand the borders of Greece, nationalists had to prove historic right of territories beyond the presence of "Greeks" abroad. This was largely achieved by documenting, dating and preserving "ruins," and antique objects that predated the modern Greek state. The creation of an archaeological record in order to connect the past to the present was ultimately used to "establish political legitimacy" in claiming territories beyond the established borders.[157] Despite the presence of cultural hybrids present all throughout the territories which Greece wished to encompass, nationalist narratives were created to reinforce the legitimacy of their borders focused on "the image of Greek ethnic homogeneity."[158] This "pure Greek" image was also further disseminated by a state-sponsored Greek educational system.[159] The main text used in schools was *History of the Greek Nation* by Paparrigopoulos, and focused on proving "the existence of an uninterrupted continuity between the ancient Greeks, Byzantine Empire

---

[156] Agnew, 408.
[157] Agnew, 411.
[158] Agnew, 412.
[159] Agnew, 412.

and modern Greeks" in order to bolster territorial claims
(much as the Turks did as well).[160]

One of the biggest proponents of irredentist policy
was eventual prime minister Eleutherios Venizelos. As a
part of the victorious Entente in WWI, Greece led by
Venizelos was able to negotiate through the Treaty of
Sèvres (1920) for the reincorporation of Northern Epirus,
Thrace, the islands of Imbros and Tenedos, but
Constantinople, to the Greek State.[161] This treaty also gave
Greece the control of the Turkish port city of Smyrna in
order to protect the ethnic-Greeks in the area. While this
Greek occupation was sanctioned by the Allies, and agreed
upon by the Sultan of the Ottoman Empire, both Greece
and Turkey failed to ratify it into law resulting in the
outbreak of the Greco-Turkish War (1919-1922). Despite
the treaty of Sèvres only sanctioning the Greek army's
presence in Smyrna, forces continued to push east towards
Ankara to crush Kemalist forces. Ultimately, the Hellenic
Army was defeated in the battle at the Sakarya River, and
pushed the Turkish National Assembly to select Mustafa
Kemal as commander-in-chief, Field Marshal and *Ghazi*.[162]

Once defeated, the Hellenic Army retreated back
towards Izmir and the coast. As military discipline broke
down and Turkish irregulars harassed their flanks, reports
of violence perpetrated by the Hellenic Army surfaced.
Notably, Arthur Toynbee "criticized the Hellenic Army for

---

[160] Malešević, "Did Wars Make Nation-States in the Balkans?: Nationalisms, Wars and States in the 19th and Early 20th Century South East Europe," 321.
[161] Hofmann, Bjørnlund, and Meichanetsidis, *The Genocide of the Ottoman Greeks*, 444.
[162] Mazower, *Salonica, City of Ghosts*, 319.

'a ruthless warfare against the Turkish population.'"[163] A "deficit in the research" pertaining to the conduct of Greek armed forces in Asia Minor from 1919-1922 has been noted by historians; though it is generally accepted that violence did occur on both sides (Greek and Turkish).[164] What is important to note is that despite the violence perpetrated by Hellenic forces, the victims of the genocide in Turkey cannot be held responsible for the "real or alleged crimes of a third state."[165] Meaning, that regardless of the violence perpetrated by the Greek Army, their actions cannot be used to justify the violence against ethnic-Greeks in the area.

On October 25, 1920 the Greek King, Alexander, suddenly died from blood poisoning when his pet monkey bit him.[166] The death of King Alexander plus mounting tensions within Greece between the Royalists and Venizelists (Liberal Party), due to international conflicts, triggered a shift in political support. After the November 1920 elections, monarchists regained a majority in parliament and recalled the former King, Constantine (Alexander's father). As a result of this, Elefterios

[163] Mazower, 320; Hofmann, Bjørnlund, and Meichanetsidis, *The Genocide of the Ottoman Greeks*, 8–9.
[164] Hofmann, Bjørnlund, and Meichanetsidis, *The Genocide of the Ottoman Greeks*, 8.
[165] Hofmann, Bjørnlund, and Meichanetsidis, 8.
[166] Editors of Encyclopedia Britannica, *Alexander,* Encyclopedia Britannica, https://www.britannica.com/biography/Alexander-king-of-Greece, Accessed March 2018.

Venizelos, the now former prime minister, left the country.[167]

Venizelos' abrupt departure led to a disengagement of the Allied forces, and a withdrawal of their military support from both Smyrna and the Greeks in Turkey. After this defeat the Greek government decided to withdraw all troops from Smyrna between August 26 and September 8, 1922. By August 31, 1922, Kemalist forces had set fire to the Christian quarters of Smyrna, and the systematic killing of Greeks continued unabated. It was not until the Greek-Turkish convention of Lausanne on January 30, 1923 that both parties agreed to an obligatory population exchange, and that the atrocities subsided.[168] Additionally, after the Hellenic Army's defeat and retreat from the outskirts of Ankara, Greek irredentist policy was effectively abandoned and the government instead focused on the settling of hundreds of thousands of ethnic-Greek refugees now within their borders.

---

[167] Tessa Hofmann, Matthias Bjørnlund, and Vasileios Meichanetsidis, *The Genocide of the Ottoman Greeks* (New York: Aristide D. Caratzas, 2011), 435; Hofmann, Bjørnlund, and Meichanetsidis, *The Genocide of the Ottoman Greeks*, 435.
[168] Hofmann, Bjørnlund, and Meichanetsidis, *The Genocide of the Ottoman Greeks*, 435–37.

Nationalism in the Nicomedia Region:

As a part of the Ottoman Empire, the Greek subjects of Nicomedia (and Anatolia in general) lived in a society where "religion and aristocratic lineage" not cultural differences determined your social in/exclusion.[169] This stratification of society along lines of religion was established by the rulers who used Islamic doctrine to rule over subjects using the "relatively segregated confessional communities—millets."[170] Millets were run by high ranking members of the clergy that were responsible for handing legal matters within their community and as such had the legal system at their disposal. The Greek Orthodox Christians were part of the Rum millet, which was inclusive of all Orthodox Christians, not just Greeks. However, it was members of the Greek Orthodox clergy that held many high ranking positions.

What is important to note in this society was the fluidity that existed in how people identified. Before the 1850s social mobility "implied acculturation into the *ethnie*" that was associated with the division of labor in which you partook.[171] As a result there was overlap between class and ethnic background. For example, labels such as "Serb," "Bulgar" or other "Slav" implied peasant status while joining the merchant class in town meant "becoming a 'Greek.'"[172] Further, until the mid-nineteenth

---

[169] Malešević, "Did Wars Make Nation-States in the Balkans?: Nationalisms, Wars and States in the 19th and Early 20th Century South East Europe," 316.
[170] Malešević, 316.
[171] Malešević, 316.
[172] Malešević, 316.

century Greek was considered to be the language of the upper middle Christian classes and led most of them to identify as Greek. This however is not indicative of a "willingness to support the establishment of an independent Greek state."[173] The concept of "Greekness" at the time was a "status category" one could claim via class mobility.[174]

   As established earlier, the spread of nationalist ideas in the early nineteenth century Balkans was slow moving, and in reality was a "confused, unarticulated set of ideas shared by a...small number of, mostly upper middle class" that were interested in either reformation of or overthrowing Ottoman rule in order to establish a "Christian pan-Balkan polity."[175] What is important to note is that the influential or wealthy Christians and clergy of the Orthodox Church in the Ottoman Empire were uninterested in the destruction of it as they enjoyed their political privilege and religious autonomy.[176] On the other hand, Christian peasants were more interested in simply surviving regardless of whether their "overlords" were Christian or Muslims, both of whom were equally "unbearable.[177]" Furthermore, even once the secular ideas of Enlightenment and Romanticism began to reach the Balkan region religious and cultural life continued to be subject to "religious and confessional worldviews." This

---

[173] Malešević, 316.
[174] Malešević, 316; Agnew, "No Borders, No Nations: Making Greece in Macedonia," 405.
[175] Malešević, 317.
[176] Malešević, 317.
[177] Malešević, 317.

meant that those that first began to rebel did so not along lines of nationalism but rather of "religious millenarianism" by way of a new Christian Kingdom.[178]

The fluidity of ethnicity that characterized this region is exactly the reason that nationalization in the Balkans took a violent turn. This fluidity evident not only in ethnic identification, but also in shared social practices and linguistic hybridity. All of which "worked against the drawing of clear borderlines."[179] These fuzzy lines of distinction were thus combated by national activists who used violence to force local people to choose sides and thus led to the creation of modern ethnic identities.[180] Violence breeds violence, thus in using violence as a method to force ethnic associations it only makes sense that those whom were the subjects of violence at the hands of Greek or Turkish nationalists would turn to similar tactics in seeking revenge or in establishing dominance of their particular community.

As stated previously, scholars have determined that the removal of all Christian minorities in Turkey was largely due to a governmental push for a homogenous Muslim population—for the creation of a "Turkey for the Turks."[181] This process was undertaken by the failing Ottoman Government in Constantinople, in conjunction with the rising nationalist government in Ankara headed by Mustafa Kemal. While the overall policies that dictated the

---

[178] Malešević, 318.

[179] Agnew, "No Borders, No Nations: Making Greece in Macedonia," 405.

[180] Agnew, 405.

[181] Uğur Ümit Üngör, *The Making of Modern Turkey: Nation and State in Eastern Anatolia, 1913-1950* (Oxford: Oxford University Press, 2011).

legality and general process of the removal of the Christian minorities came from the national government, the specific details of removal were left up to the regional administrators. Regional administrators such as *kaymakam* (district governor) or leaders of irregular gangs decided when particular towns were to be targeted and how they were to be destroyed. Thus, the strategies employed by the perpetrators varied widely. In the case of the Nicomedia Massacres, the two names referred to most often in the accounts relayed by Faltaits were Cemal of Nikaia and Giaour Ali. Ali, also known as the "Heathen," whose cruelty proceeded him throughout the region, and who was a professional murderer that received his commands directly from the Kemalist leaders. [182]

---

[182] "Prologue," in *The Genocide of the Greeks in Turkey: Survivor Testimonies From The Nicomedia (Izmit) Massacres of 1920-1921* (River Vale, NJ, 2016), 22; 23.

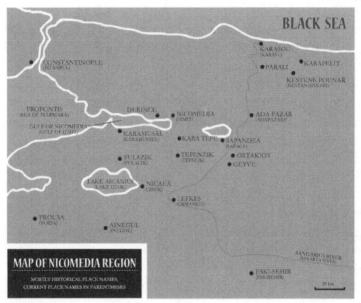

MAP OF NICOMEDIA REGION

MOSTLY HISTORICAL PLACE NAMES,
CURRENT PLACE NAMES IN PARENTHESES

183

The Massacres of Nicomedia were conducted by the aforementioned and other regional leaders under their command. In enlisting men like Ali, the Kemalist regime made it clear that they were not interested in a humane removal of the Greek Christian minority. While Kemalist leaders did have regular armed forces at their disposal, they also recruited and used violent irregular *chettes* (gangs) to remove Greeks. Additionally, various survivors interviewed by Faltaits reported Turkish peasants from villages surrounding Nicea, Kara Tepe, and Konzes, and

---

[183] Olan Wactor, *Map of Nicomedia (Izmit) Region* (The Genocide Research Center, n.d.), http://greek-genocide.net/index.php/component/content/article?id=269:the-genocide-of-the-greeks-in-turkey.

came to partake in the sacking of the Greek towns.[184] The involvement of Turkish peasants was likely the result of jealousy and a deep-seated desire for revenge against the Greeks which can be traced back to the late-eighteenth/early-nineteenth century. During this time the Turkish-Muslim peasants failed to modernize in comparison to the Christian peasantry who continued to rise in socio-economic status eventually becoming dominant players in the Ottoman economy despite their minority status.[185] Despite their inferior economic status a precarious status-quo held because Turkish peasants enjoyed superior social status as Muslims. This initial division combined with the violence of both Balkan Wars and pressures of nationalists on both sides can help to explain why and how ordinary people did terrible things. If the peasants of surrounding villages were told to resent or blame the Greeks for all of their economic shortcomings, for the wars, for the violence raging in the region—this would have been enough to push ordinary people to great violence.

Due to the diverse ethnic groups that lived in relative harmony for centuries under the banner of the Ottoman Empire the would-be perpetrators of genocide had to first convince a particular group of their superior status

[184] Faltaits, *The Genocide of the Greeks in Turkey: Survivor Testimonies From The Nicomedia (Izmit) Massacres of 1920-1921*, 59,66-67, 77, 93.
[185] George N. Shirinian, *The Asia Minor Catastrophe and the Ottoman Greek Genocide*, 12–13.

as the "in-group" or "the people."[186] This was done in a number of ways as discussed previously, but the slogan "Turkey for the Turks" is an example of nationalist propaganda created with the intent of othering. For when one group holds the "in-group" title, all further groups are automatically deemed *other* and therefore as outside of their "universe of obligation," as "less than fully human," as "infidels" or "giaours" (non-believers).[187] Thus, by the Turkish government deeming Turkey only for Muslim Turks, all other ethnic and/or religious minorities were deemed "the enemy...[that] must be eliminated"— particularly Christians.[188]

The events at Nicomedia show exactly how the Turks employed genocidal violence in an effort to destroy the Greek's community ties and sense of identity in order to create a homogeneous Turkish center in Anatolia. This forced relocation of ethnic-Greeks ultimately resulted in genocide that was perpetrated by both regular and irregular Turkish forces as well as peasants from the surrounding areas. By attacking institutions and groups of people that were valued with-in the communities compliance was guaranteed. In the following section through the analysis of attacks on religious institutions and clergy as well as attacks on women and children, the extent, brutality and

---

[186] Jones, *Genocide: A Comprehensive Introduction*, 4; Frank Robert Chalk, Kurt Jonassohn, and Montreal Institute for Genocide Studies, *The History and Sociology of Genocide: Analyses and Case Studies* (New Haven: Yale University Press, 1990), 28.
[187] Helen Fein, "Genocide: A Sociological Perspective," in *Genocide: An Anthropological Reader*, ed. Alexander Laban Hinton (Malden: Blackwell Publishers, 2002), 74–90; Chalk, Jonassohn, and Montreal Institute for Genocide Studies, *The Hisory and Sociology of Genocide,* 28.
[188] Fein, "Genocide: A Sociological Perspective," 74-90.

effectiveness of removal policy via nationalist rhetoric can be seen.

Violence Against Churches, Clergy, and the Faithful

Superiority of religion was used as a mechanism to
destroy communities in different ways depending on the
particular group in question. For example, Turkish peasants
used religion to justify the crimes committed in the sacking
of towns and villages. On the other hand, members of the
Turkish regular army and state hired irregular gangs used
religion to dehumanize the Greeks. The military and *chetes*
employed torture tactics of gross violence that targeted
men, women, children and the elderly alike in an effort to
break their spirt. Turkey's ultimate goal was to remove all
Greeks from Anatolia. This can be seen in a secret order
sent on May 14, 1914 from the Turkish Minister of Internal
Affairs, Talaat. The memo states that all Greek residents on
the Asia Minor coast must "be forced to vacate their
villages and to be settled…in their determined places."
Should they refuse, he continues, "please give oral
instructions to brother Muslims, for the purpose of forcing
the Greeks, *be every kind of actions, to be expatriated
voluntarily"* (emphasis added).[189] This order gave anyone
operating in conjunction with the Turkish government,
whether a regular soldier or a brigand, the latitude to
remove Greeks in any way they deemed fit. Ultimately, this
culminated in what we today know as genocidal violence.

---

[189] Talaat, "Secret Order of the Turkish Minister of Internal Affairs, Talaat, Dated 14th
May, 1914," in *At Last We Uprooted Them: The Genocide of Greeks of Pontos, Thrace
and Asia Minor Through French Archives* (Thessaloniki: Publishing House Kyriakidis
Brothers s.a., n.d.), 107.

By attacking the Greek Orthodox Church, which was and continues to be central to Greek culture/life, Greeks were being hit in a more subtle way. By attacking the institution that was at the center of their lives in terms of culture, community, family, tradition, language—Turks were attacking their identity as Greeks. By committing acts of sacrilege in churches, attacking communities on major feast days, humiliating/mutilating clergy, disrespecting the dead, and through forced assimilation, Turks sought to dismantle the identity of the Greeks in order to dissolve their communities in Asia Minor and to create a homogeneous Muslim Turkey.[190]

To the religiously devout, churches and places of worship in general are considered to be safe places. Historically, they are where people seek political asylum, food, shelter, money, first aid and the list goes on. By specifically targeting their place of worship and turning it into a place of fear, death and destruction the Turks looked to break Greek faith, and thus their sprit to make them more willing to cooperate. This took a variety of forms changing in severity depending on the particular town or village. For example when the Turks entered Ortakioy at the end of March 1920, their first order of business was to burn down "half the city" and the "great Church of Saint Nicholas." On the other hand, in Fulazik, 300 men and boys over the age of fourteen were gathered, locked and set on fire, in the Church of Saint George. Once locked inside the trapped

---

[190] Testimony of Pavlos Balidis, "Fulazik," in *The Genocide of the Greeks in Turkey,* ed. Kostas Faltaits (River Vale: Cosmos Publishing, 2016), 48-50; Testimony of Eleni Vafiadis, "Lefkes" in Faltaits, 84.

men were forced to use sacred objects, like icons, to break through the doors to survive. In this case the Turks not only desecrated the church, but they forced the Greeks to take an active role in that desecration or die.[191]

Other instances, such as in the case of the Church of Saint Constantine in Karasou, where approximately sixty men were gathered, were threatened and held at gun point while the Turks shook them down for valuables/cash. In his testimony Alexios Karaselidis recalled thinking, "Inside the church, we were in the hands of the Turks." The considerations here are interesting because as previously stated, before outbreak of violence, the church would have been a place to escape from the Turks, a safe haven. By internally admitting that the church in Karasou no longer belonged to him or his community, but rather to the Turks, we can see the beginning phases of disconnection of identity from place. This disconnection from place would only increase the more heinous the action. For example, in Nicaea, men and women were gathered into the Church of the Holy Virgin, "and there they were literally butchered into pieces." At this point when the home/communities of the Greeks were in imminent danger of complete destruction, and was no longer defensible, the will to survive overpowered the sense of identity and allegiance to the community; so, they fled or attempted to. I say attempt here intentionally. Many Greeks realized early on what was happening in their towns and/or had heard news from surrounding towns that had been attacked. So when Turks

---

[191] Testimony of Pavlos Balidis, "Fulazik," in Faltaits, 49.

were spotted they would try to leave (sometimes immediately), but the Turks did not allow this. They would gather up the fleeing Greeks from the surrounding mountains or villages and either kill them on the spot or bring them back to their town for torture/slaughter/rape.[192]

The Greek Orthodox faith celebrates a wide variety of feast days honoring a number of things throughout the year. In the cases of some villages in Nicomedia, the Turks chose to invade, attack or both on days of great significance to the church. For example in Lefkes the Turks invaded on the "eve of the Feast of the Apostles" in 1920.[193] Later, in March 1921, Kara Tepe was invaded on the "day of the Annunciation," and was subsequently bombed.[194] In Karasou, the Turks tried to manipulate the religious Greeks by ringing the church bells on June 30, the feast day of the Apostles, after they had already fled to the mountains.[195] Thankfully this tactic did not work, but it does shed light on the lengths that the Turks were willing to go in order to catch and slaughter the Greeks who were in hiding. Overall, the attacks on a days of great religious importance was incredibly sacrilegious. These actions showed not only the depth of their disrespect for Christianity, but how superior they felt to the Greeks. This superiority complex can also be seen in the targeted attacks of the Turks on members of the clergy.

---

[192] Testimony of Alexios Karaselidis, "The Exodus of Karasou," in Faltaits, 108; Testimony of Stathis Lolosidis, "The Last Survivor of Nicaea," in Faltaits, 60.
[193] Testimony of Eleni Vafiadis, "Lefkes," in Faltaits, 81.
[194] Testimony of Dimitrios Giavridis, "Kara Tepe," in Faltaits, 65.
[195] Testimony of Alexios Karaselidis, "The Exodus of Karasou," in Faltaits, 111.

As mentioned earlier, during the Ottoman Empire the various religious minorities had the ability to govern themselves via the millet system which allowed each community to have their own schools, languages, and leaders that enforced laws and collected taxes. Under the millet system of the Ottoman Empire it was the ecumenical patriarchate and members of the clergy who oversaw the Orthodox Christians at the time. During the genocide however, that's to say once the Turkish Republic emerged, the Orthodox clergy no longer had the same political clout that they once had. Despite this, clergy members were still considered to be leaders within the Greek communities; so, when the Turks forced members of the clergy to "demand exorbitant taxes" from townspeople in Karasou, Turkey sought to leverage the trust that his proverbial flock had in him as their religious leader.[196]

Bad as it is to manipulate a community via its religious leader, it is another thing entirely to publicly humiliate members of the clergy. The most extreme case is best recounted by Pavlos Balidis from Fulazik. He explained that Father Phillipos was ordered by Kemal to round up men and boys fourteen and over and to have them meet in Church of Saint George just to "talk," and so

> Up to 300 men and boys from the ages of fourteen years and upwards were gathered inside the church of Saint George. Crying and crossing themselves they relied on Father Phillipos to comfort them and to give them Holy Communion. However the Father

---

[196] Testimony of Alexios Karaselidis, "The Exodus of Karasou," in Faltaits, 109.

had lost his voice and was unable to speak…[then
the Kemal of Karamusal entered the church and] He
jumped onto the back of Father Phillipos who by
now had a rope tied around his mouth…and
proceeded to ride Father Phillipos like a horse out
of the church pulling on the rope in the
process…[he] fainted and fell to the ground and
Kemal then cut one of the Father's eyes out…
Later, down near the little river named Tourali I saw
Father Phillipos lying in the grass, his beard
removed from his face, the bridle still in his mouth,
his clothes in tatters…his throat cut, and only a flap
of skin attaching his head to his body.[197]

In other towns, priests and their entire families (including
children and grandparents) were dragged into the streets
where they were all publicly raped, murdered and
dismembered. The Turks attacked the priest in Kara Tepe
for trying to save the holy objects from inside a church
before it burnt down;[198] in the Pringiponnisia seminary
priests had their beards shaved off by Turks and were
conscripted.[199] In these examples, all of the priests were
symbolically stripped, in one way or another of their pride,
status and authority over their communities. In Fulazik,
Father Phillipos was literally ridden like a pack animal by
the Kemal. He was dragged through the burning town, he

---

[197] Testimony of Pavlos Balidis, "Fulazik," in Faltaits, 46-51.
[198] Testimony of Dimitrios Giavridis, "Kara Tepe," in Faltaits, 66.
[199] Harry Tsirkinidis, *At Last We Uprooted Them: The Genocide of Greeks of Pontos,
Thrace and Asia Minor through French Archives*, trans. Stratos Mavrantonis
(Thessaloniki: Kyriakidis Brother Publishing House, 1999), 90, 92.

likely was forced to watch the rape of women and children, and when the Turks grew tired of him his corpse was further mutilated before being tossed into a stream.

This is extreme nationalism in action. The Turkish nationalist narrative had been so effective that not only were the Greeks considered to be *other,* but they were *unworthy giaours.* According to an internal memo from the French army, the Turks could be over heard claiming repeatedly that their "Prophet was wrong to allow freedoms to Christians…that was the cause of our misfortune. From now on we will obliterate anything that is Christian!" And so they did.[200]

After the death of a loved one, each culture has a method for disposal of the body to show respect to them, to their family to their god—or whatever the case may be. Greeks are no different. In the Orthodox Church after the death of a person, there is a church service to bless the body and the departed soul, and then a burial in a cemetery. The Turks on no occasion took any care to dispose of or bury any of the thousands of Greeks that they murdered in Nicomedia.[201] The rotting bodies of dead Greeks were left in the burnt remnants of houses, or they were thrown into rivers like the Sangarius near Ortakioy where the "water was still murky red" from the blood of the Greeks that were slaughtered.[202]

The corpses that Turks left strewn throughout the countryside and mountains of Nicomedia usually did not

---

[200] Tsirkinidis, *At Last We Uprooted Them,* 90.

[201] Faltaits, *The Genocide of the Greeks in Turkey.*

[202] Testimony of Paraskevi Anastasiadou, "The Teacher of Ortakioy," in Faltaits, 95.

get the chance to decay naturally. Generally before that could happen the Christians who were butchered "into pieces [up] to their navels" and/or that had their stomachs sliced open were strewn about and were literally left to the dogs.[203] This happened in Lefkes and in Ortakioy. In Lefkes and Ortakioy the Turkish women could be seen and heard walking the streets of the destroyed town.[204] In Ortakioy specifically, women were laughing not only at the carnage but also at the dogs eating the dismembered corpses.[205] More disturbing still in the mountains surrounding Ortakioy, Turkish peasants chased after the fleeing Greeks to hunt them with their dogs. In fact, there are accounts of the Greeks being hunted, like animals, in Ortakioy, and Karasou showing that the policies of extreme nationalism had successfully dehumanized the Greeks to the point that they were no longer human but rather animal.[206]

Perhaps the most blatant disrespect not only for the dead but for Christians in general was the use of crucifixion.[207] Historically crucifixion was the death sentence ascribed to criminals, but as most know it is the way in which Jesus, who according to the church was the son of god/the holy spirit incarnate, was killed. Christians use the symbol of the crucifix in their houses, on icons,

---

[203] Testimony of Benjamin Lazian, "Giaour Ali," in Faltaits, 100.
[204] Testimony of Eleni Vafiadis, "Lefkes" in Faltaits, 86; Testimony of Paraskevi Anastasiadou, "The Teacher of Ortakioy," in Faltaits 95.
[205] Testimony of Paraskevi Anastasiadou, "The Teacher of Ortakioy," in Faltaits, 95.
[206] Testimony of Paraskevi Anastasiadou, "The Teacher of Ortakioy," in Faltaits, 93–95.
[207] Dimitrios Giavridis, "Kara Tepe," in Faltaits, 69; Testimony of Alexios Karaselidis, "The Exodus of Karasou," in Faltaits 115.

they wear it on chains around their neck to honor the sacrifice that God made for his children in allowing his son to die. It is for this reason that it is so disrespectful. The Turks did not choose this method of murder because "Barbara Evrenglou, an elderly lady of 85 years old" was too difficult to kill using a knife or a gun, and so she was left "still gasping, crucified and nailed outside the door of her house, and [with] her eyes hanging out" because it was easier.[208] No, Barbara was crucified, like her God was, to send a message to any surviving Christians that happened to see her nailed there. The message being that Christians were weaker, inferior, and that they did not belong in Turkey, and for any Christians that they encountered this was the fate that awaited them.

---

[208] Testimony of Dimitrios Giavridis, "Kara Tepe," in Faltaits, 69.

Violence Against Women and Children

All Greeks at this time were forced to endure the heinous crimes committed against them and their communities. The attacks on each community generally followed the same pattern. First, Turks would demand money, taxes, food or valuables in order to guarantee the safety of the Greeks. Then, Turkish soldiers of the regular and irregular forces and Turkish peasants began "looting the homes" of Greeks.[209] They were forced to watch as Turks entered their homes pulled "men out by force, taking with them whatever they found." Turks went so far as to make "people remove their clothes and shoes" off their backs for them to take.[210] Then Greeks watched as all of their "belongings were loaded onto thousands of mules and horses" and dragged off to Turkish villages.[211] Sometime in between the monetary demands and the looting; the kidnapping, rape, killing and mutilation began with orders to "go straight to their [Greek] villages—women, children, whatever you find, kill it."[212]

The more that the Greeks were pushed into the category of *other* by the Turkish government, Kemalist leadership, soldiers and peasants, the less human Greeks became. The more marginalized the Greeks became, the less of a threat they posed especially as the genocide proceeded. With each successful attack and complete

---

[209] Testimony of Eleni Vafiadis, "Lefkes," in Faltaits, 83-89.
[210] Testimony of Pavlos Balidis, "Fulazik," in Faltaits, 47.
[211] Testimony of Pavlos Balidis, "Fulazik," in Faltaits, 47.
[212] Testimony of Alexios Karaselidis, "The Exodus of Karasou," in Faltaits, 114.

destruction of a number of towns the Turks felt more
empowered in their actions, and more confident in the
violence committed against Greeks which lead them to
become increasingly violent.

Despite the earlier focus on members of the clergy,
women were in no way excluded. They were often raped in
front of their husbands and children, mutilated, taken for
harems, sold to slavery and/or killed. In Fulazik, Nicaea,
Kara Tepe, Konzes, Lefkes and Ortakioy survivors reported
the sounds of "musical instruments being played"[213] and
hearing Turks "croon[ing] grossly offensive songs"[214]
while women were forced to remove all of their clothes and
dance naked for the soldiers who would sing and play the
oud before they were tortured and killed.[215]

Music was a constant in Turks town-to-town
massacres. Survivors reported that they could hear
"[with]in the clamor" as bullets were being fired, and
buildings were in flames, a "weeping that rose to the
heavens, [and] the ouds of the Turks and their singing."[216]
It would seem that despite all of the death and destruction
surrounding them the Turks found time to enjoy
themselves. Within what most survivors of these atrocities
would later call "hell," the Turks acted as if they were at a
festival that should be enjoyed complete with dancers,
music, singing and fineries. The dancers of course, were
prisoners of war and were Greek women and children

[213] Testimony of Pavlos Balidis, "Fulazik," in Faltaits, 50.
[214] Testimony of Paraskevi Anastasiadou, "The Teacher of Ortakioy," in Faltaits, 92.
[215] Testimony of Eleni Vafiadis, "Lefkes," in Faltaits, 86.
[216] Testimony of Eleni Vafiadis, "Lefkes," in Faltaits, 86.

forced to dance naked for the entertainment of the Turks.[217] Additionally, the fineries used during these celebrations were stolen. In many cases these objects (usually gold) were taken *out* of dead bodies that had either been cut open to the intestines, or dug out of the ashes of bodies to find things that had been swallowed by their victims.[218] Music can also be understood as a way to celebrate victory over the Greeks.

The use of music in these orgy like settings is interesting in attempting to understand the motivation of the Turks. Perhaps the music was a way to distract from what was actually happening around them. The music could have been used to transport the perpetrators to a euphoric place where they were surrounded with only fine things and an abundant amount of women at their disposal. Music could also have been used in order to help the atrocities move along. Equally important to consider is that quite possibly some of the Turks were sadistic and thus did enjoy committing these genocidal acts. In this case, by celebrating what they had achieved through violence the Turks were solidifying their success and victory over the dirty *giaours* that plagued Turkey.

Victory seems out of place in discussing the wholesale massacre or genocide of a group of people. To the Turks, however, that is what it was, a victory over the infidel. A way for Turks to claim the dominance of the Islamic faith over Christianity, that they imagined they deserved due to nationalist rhetoric at the time. These

---

[217] Testimony of Yiannis Valaris, "The Songs of Fulazik," in Faltaits, 55.

[218] Testimony of Poimenarch Stephan Hovakimian, "The Armenians," in Faltaits, 105.

actions were the physical manifestation of the Turkish people claiming the land based on the nationalist rhetoric which told them they were entitled to. This entitlement therefore allowed them to be rid of the *giaours* who had squatted on their land for so long, by any means necessary. Their grossly overkill actions successfully dehumanized the Greeks by reducing their resolve to live, and by forcing women into impossible circumstances where their only concern was survival.

To some Greek women and girls, a fate worse than death was the prospect of being "taken," married off, forced to bear children, or to be forcibly converted to Islam (or all of the above).[219] Yet these were some of the choices that many, mostly girls, faced. Conversion to Islam, if offered at all, was offered as *a choice*.[220] The other choice being death for the crime of being a *giaour*. This was the case in Lefkes where after surviving the initial waves of slaughter, the remaining Christians were told that "they had to become Turks if they wanted to survive."[221] So they became Turks by changing their names and wearing traditional Turkish garb, the women covered their faces, and their youth were married according to the Quran.[222] If you were found to still have Christian leanings, like Yiangos was during a surprise search that revealed a small

[219] Testimony of Paraskevi Anastasiadou, "The Teacher of Ortaioy," in Faltaits, 96.
[220] Testimony of Eleni Vafiadis, "Lefkes," in Faltaits, 84; Testimony of Paraskevi Anastasiadou, "The Teacher of Ortakioy," in Faltaits 94–97.
[221] Testimony of Eleni Vafiadis, "Lefkes," in Faltaits, 84.
[222] Testimony of Eleni Vafiadis, "Lefkes," in Faltaits, 84.

icon tucked away in his pocket, you were killed after you dug your own grave.[223]

Often times the young girls who were taken from their families to be married off to Turks was agreed to for the sake of survival, and with the hope of a future escape.[224] Simply put, Greek women and girls did what was needed in order to survive despite the many atrocities they were forced to endure. In most villages the "young and beautiful women," the "prettiest young women," "the most beautiful girls," were the first to be taken from their homes and families by Turkish regular and irregular soldiers for sex.[225]

Some young women/girls were gathered up and taken to be part of a harem or if found to be too old, forced into slavery.[226] Other women, including children and the elderly, were not so lucky. According to Stathis Lolosidis in Nicaea beginning at dawn and lasting until noon "women—starting with little girls of six years old to elderly women—they would rape and then slaughter…and [then] they butchered and turned human flesh into tiny little pieces."[227] The mutilation and dismemberment of the females after their rape is symbolic of their distaste for Greek Christians and their determination to rid Turkey of them. By attacking young women who are of child bearing

---

[223] Testimony of Eleni Vafiadis, "Lefkes," in Faltaits, 84.
[224] Testimony of Paraskevi Anastasiadou, "The Teacher of Ortakioy," in Faltaits, 94–97.
[225] Testimony of Eleni Vafiadis, "Lefkes," in Faltaits, 87; Testimony of Christos Kalantzis, "Fountoukia," in Faltaits 73; Testimony of Stathis Lolosidis, "The Last Survivor of Nicaea," in Faltaits 59.
[226] Testimony of Stathis Lolosidis, "The Last Survivor of Nicaea," in Faltaits, 59; Testimony of Paraskevi Anastasiadou, "The Teacher of Ortakioy," in Faltaits 95.
[227] Testimony of Stathis Lolosidis, "The Last Survivor of Nicaea," in Faltaits, 63.

age they ensure that no more Greeks are born in Turkey, thus snuffing out the population there. Further by "slaughtering them and by torturing them heinously" the established their dominance as Turkish men over Greek men who were rendered useless in protecting their mothers, wives and children.[228] The rape and murder of elderly women served a similar purpose. By attacking the elders of families, the Turks sent the message that all aspects of Greek culture and tradition were null and void, their *other* status solidified. Community and cultural hierarchies were no longer valid as they were no longer considered human or a part of the *in group* that needed to be protected.

Women at times attempted to appeal to the better nature of Turks begging for their mercy. In Lefkes, a young woman by the name of Rodanthe Paschalidis was overheard saying to a pair of Turks: "'Don't ruin my life. I have not yet lived enough in this world.'"[229] Her appeal to the Turk was met by a missed gunshot which prompted her to respond that she was "'not a creature that you can just kill.'"[230] Her insubordination as a *giaour* was met by "another Turk stabb[ing] her with his knife" to silence her once and for all as if to prove that yes, she was a creature that could simply be killed.[231] The method used to silence Paschalidis, though it showed a disregard for Greek lives, was relatively subdued. Meaning that she was killed quickly and was not subjected to torture tactics before she

---

Testimony of Christos Kalantzis, "Fountoukia," in Faltaits, 73.

[229] Testimony of Eleni Vafiadis, "Lefkes," in Faltaits, 85.

[230] Testimony of Eleni Vafiadis, "Lefkes," in Faltaits, 85.

[231] Testimony of Eleni Vafiadis, "Lefkes," in Faltaits, 85.

was killed. She was stabbed, her life ended, her voice silenced.

In other cases Greek women would beg "'don't kill us by torturing us...kill us quickly,'" but were not granted a clean and quick death.[232] In Lefkes, likely Paschalidis' friends and family, women were "toyed with" by the Turks. The Turks raped and then "would cut out their nipples of their breasts passing them around and playing with them like a *komboloi* (worry beads), and then would kill the women by torturing them horribly."[233] This drawn out process of rape, torture, murder and mutilation of Greek women was another way to not only dehumanize them, but to declare their dominance as Muslim Turks and to break down Greek ties to Turkey. In their torture of Christians, Turks were reinforcing the idea that only they, the Muslim Turks, belonged in the country. By specifically targeting women, they render Greeks incapable of reproduction and further underscoring their goal of ultimate annihilation of identity and culture.

The Turkish attempts to render Greeks as insignificant and inferior beings that had no place in the new Turkey is incredibly clear in the instances where Greeks were forced to bear witness to the rape and murder of each other. The first night of the Turkish attacks in Fountokila, women and girls "the age of ten and over" were raped in front of their mothers while "the young[er] ones [were forced to] hold candles to illuminate them."[234] This

[232] Testimony of Eleni Vafiadis, "Lefkes," in Faltaits, 86.
[233] Testimony of Eleni Vafiadis, "Lefkes," in Faltaits, 86.
[234] Testimony of Christos Kalantzis, "Fountoukia," in Faltaits, 73.

forced participation reinforced the inferiority of Greeks to the young children by making them an active participant in the torture of their mothers, sisters and friends. The absolute control and perceived superiority of the Turks can further be seen in the case of Haralambos Sevastou, who was caught hiding in the mountains outside of Lefkes with his three daughters. Once caught, the Turks "cut off his two front legs to the knees and took out one of his eyes," rendering him physically incapacitated. Then, to further emphasize his forced subservience and unworthiness as a Greek, the Turks "placed his daughters in his lap, and beheaded them all [one by one] in this way."[235] Here we see the implied and supposed superiority of the Turks based on the nationalist propaganda at the time physically reinforced. It was not enough to simply kill Sevastou and his family to show their inferiority to the Turks. Sevastou first had to be severely maimed, to the point where he could no longer protect his children, and he was then forced to watch as they were killed. Killed not just in front of him forcing him to bear witness, but physically on him. With no possible way to fight back the Turks continued to crush the spirit or the Greeks and to eradicate not only their communities but their culture in Turkey.

The deconstruction and obliteration of Greek communities was furthered by the killing of children. By first killing Greek women and then Greek children, Turks attempted to ensure that no aspect of Greek culture could continue. In some towns, the killing of children was

---

[235] Testimony of Eleni Vafiadis, "Lefkes," in Faltaits, 87.

relatively straight forward. For example in Fulazik the children were buried alive and in Lefkes the Turks "smashed the children's heads" in.[236] In the towns of Fulazik, Kara Tepe, Fountoukilia, Lefkes, Ortakioy and Karasou the killing of children was forced upon the Greeks themselves.

While their towns were under attack, Greeks found themselves facing the choice of saving themselves or saving their children. When Turks invaded towns Greeks attempted to flee, and hid in a number of places ranging from the mountains to the sewers.[237] Hordes of men, women and children fled from the violence of the Turks. Once in hiding small children and infants could be heard "crying from hunger."[238] Out of fear of "their cries…giving away their location,"[239] Kalantzis explained that "we killed our children so they would not betray us…and thus bringing the Turks upon us."[240] How small children were killed depended on the particular circumstances of the family.

Some children were quite literally abandoned in bushes as families fled from their homes and towns that were up in flames and under attack. In Kara Tepe Dimitrios Giavridis explains that he was initially separated from his family, but once the Turks had deserted the carcass of Kara

---

[236] Testimony of Yiannis Valaris, "The Songs of Fulazik," in Faltaits, 55; Testimony of Eleni Vafiadis, "Lefkes," in Faltaits 85.
[237] Testimony of Christos Kalantzis, "Fountoukia," in Faltaits, 73; Testimony of Eleni Vafiadis, "Lefkes," in Faltaits, 85.
[238] Testimony of Pavlos Balidis, "Fulazik," in Faltaits, 51.
[239] Testimony of Alexios Karaselidis, "The Exodus of Karasou," in Faltaits, 115.
[240] Testimony of Christos Kalantzis, "Fountoukia," in Faltaits, 73.

Tepe, he ventured to find those that had escaped into the surrounding area. As he descended from a ravine Giavridis,

> Heard crying and I saw my infant child thrown into some branches. I picked up the child and brought him to [a nearby town] Faktori where I found more people including my wife from whom I learned that she had thrown him away to save the other two older children. [241]

Other small children were given opium to quiet them so they would not give away the location of those in hiding. But this opium was not always on hand, or it was not in large supply because in many cases "mothers…gave them large doses of opium and thus killed" their children.[242] The choice placed before these women that of self-preservation and safety of the community or the life of their child, could not have been an easy one and in some cases was beyond their control.

Some mothers attempted to save the lives of their children for as long as they possibly could, but other community members that feared for their lives stepped in. Such was the case of Eleni Vafiadis from Lefkes who found herself and ten other Greeks hiding in the sewers under the town's toilets. Above them they could hear the sounds of slaughter, and the "cries of small children" being killed by the Turks. All the while, she clutched her infant to her hoping that they would not be found and that they would survive. But, after a few days

---

[241] Testimony of Dimitrios Giavridis, "Kara Tepe," in Faltaits, 68–69.
[242] Testimony of Paraskevi Anastasiadou, "The Teacher of Ortakioy," in Faltaits, 93.

In the sewers I was half conscious from the horrible odour. I had in my lap my baby which started to cry and the other women said: 'He will betray us with his cries.' Then one woman, Athena Hadzi, took my child from my lap, squeezed its neck tightly, strangled it, and then gave it back to me lifeless...We stayed there five days and five nights...[All the while] I had my dead child in my lap and I saw the worms starting to eat its little eyes. My body was completely numb.[243]

The psychological effects of watching your child decay in your arms, as you yourself are starving and in fear for your life, can only be immense. As discussed later on, survivors of this Genocide did not speak of their experiences for many years, I can only imagine that it was at least partially a result of not wanting to relive such devastating experiences such as killing your child. I cannot say definitively that Turks intended for Greeks to kill their own offspring, but it must have come as a welcome discovery. Not only would it have been less for them to do, but it again forced Greeks into the position of helping to destroy their communities and families. Further, by forcing them to take an active role in the expulsion of Greeks they underscored the inferiority of their lives and the superiority of Turkish ones. Thus successfully dismantling Greek communities and ties to their homeland. In spite of all this,

---

[243] Testimony of Eleni Vafiadis, "Lefkes," in Faltaits, 86–87.

the Turks did not succeed in the erasure of the unique Greek culture and heritage that was present in Asia Minor.

These traumas from torture, mutilation, rape, sacrilege and the many more not discussed here—did cause the Greek communities in Asia Minor to dissolve completely, but did not break their will to survive. This can be seen in the extreme measures taken by Greeks in the Nicomedia region who willingly killed their children, were sold off into slavery, sent to labor camps, to harems, hid in sewers, and much more. Their will to first survive, and second to bear witness through the retelling of their stories so that they would not be forgotten; is a testament to the strength of Greeks of Asia Minor. Further, their descendants' will to preserve and perpetuate the memories of this atrocity as well as their dedication to the preservation of their history in culture not only in Greece but also in the U.S. is a testament to their strength of character and culture.

CHAPTER III

RESILIANCE: PRESERVATION OF CULTURE, HERITAGE AND RELIGION IN THE UNITED STATES

The atrocities that the Greeks of Asia Minor were forced to endure during their expulsion from Turkey constituted a genocide. Entire communities were destroyed, families were torn apart and all were displaced. Very few were allowed to stay in Turkey, but the majority were forced to settle in countries that were foreign to them. Despite this, these ethnic-Greeks were able to retain elements of their unique culture and language to pass down to their children and grandchildren. In this chapter, I will explore the various institutions, societies and organizations that endeavor to preserve the culture and heritage of the Greeks from Asia Minor.

Refugees of the Greek Genocide typically settled in various cities/towns/villages on the peninsula of Greece, like Kokkinia outside of Piraeus. Immigrants in those communities sought to assimilate into Greek society while still maintaining their unique experience privately and within their own homes.[244] Once in Greece immigrants from Asia Minor faced discrimination from their fellow Greeks and were called *karamalides* or *prosfiyes* when

---

[244] Renée Hirschon, *Heirs of the Greek Catastrophe: The Social Life of Asia Minor Refugees in Piraeus* (Oxford: Berghahn Books, 1998).

recognized by their Turkish accent.[245] This was largely due to the fact that most of these refugees spoke Turkey more fluently than they did Greek, and in some cases spoke no Greek at all.[246] As a result, these "Anatolian Christians" or "Christians from the East" were considered to be second class citizens and not fully Greek.[247] Fortunately as time moved forward and the next generation was born relations between ethnic-Greeks from Turkey and Greeks from Greece began to smooth. Helen Mavromatis, born to Ermofili and Yiannis Avitoglou refugees from Tokat and Ankara, Turkey, recounts that

> My grandmother didn't speak any Greek, and my mother had an accent…she used to mix up the feminine and masculine. My father was better, the only thing he had an accent. And most of the people that they came from Turkey at that time, you could recognize them because of their accent, when they spoke Greek…there was a lot of discrimination at that time toward the refugees from the local Greeks…[but] to tell you the truth, me, as I was growing up…like twenty thirty years later…I didn't feel much…between us kids, there wasn't any.[248]

It was this new generation of Greek born, Turkish descendants that would immigrate to the United States in

---

[245] Helen Mavromatis, Family and Personal History, audio recording, April 3, 2017. *Karamalides* was slang to identify someone that was from Asia Minor/Turkey, while *prosfiyes* was a demeaning way of referring to a refugee.

[246] Mazower, *Salonica: City of Ghosts,* 336–37.

[247] Mavromatis, Family and Personal History; Mazower, *Salonika: City of Ghosts,* 337.

[248] Mavromatis, Family and Personal History.

the mid-to-late twentieth century in search of better opportunities. This immigration to the US lead them also to bring the rich social culture and heritage of their homeland.[249]

Much like victims of the Holocaust, survivors of the Greek Genocide did not talk about what they suffered at the hands of their oppressors, and if they did recount their experience it was not until much later.[250] For example, Thea Halo, who wrote a narrative of her mother's experience, discloses at the beginning of her book that she had no idea what her mother suffered until well into her adult life.[251] Some accounts were recorded by historic societies and organizations in Greece, but few exist in the U.S. and in English. Despite this, in the U.S. descendants of survivors hold firm to their belief that "people **must** know what happened," and "by not recognizing and remembering those that suffered and those that died, their memories and sacrifices disappear."[252] In an effort to lift the silence of older generations, to preserve the memory of their ancestors and to educate nationally and internationally a number of organizations have been established.

Once in the US Greek immigrants, in general, attempted to establish places where the cultural norms that they were accustomed to could flourish. Early immigrants

---

[249] Theodore Saloutos, *The Greeks in the United States* (Cambridge, Mass: Harvard University Press, 1964), 1.

[250] Mazower, "Homage to Salonika," 338.

[251] Halo, *Not Even My Name*.

[252] Sandy J Papadopoulos, Greek Genocide Survivor Descendants Interview, Transcript, March 4, 2018; George Palaidis, Greek Genocide Survivor Descendants Interview, Transcript, March 7, 2018.

established coffeehouses that served as a "recreation center," providing a place to socialize with other Greeks in the immediate or neighboring community.[253] As time went on, churches took on a more prominent role in preservation of culture and heritage by establishing programs and activities that encouraged "a special community spirit." The church "sponsored schools, social events, [and] church programs" including Greek school and traditional dance.[254]

---

[253] Theodore Saloutos, *The Greeks in the United States*, 78.
[254] Saloutos, 71.

The Church and Independent Societies

The Greek Orthodox Archdiocese of America was not established officially until 1922, up until then Greek Orthodox Churches sprang up around the country. The first permeant community was founded in 1892 in New York City, at what is now the Archdiocesan Cathedral of the Holy Trinity. As of 2017 there are over 540 Parishes, 800 priests and approximately 1.5 million members of the Greek Orthodox Church in the U.S.[255] While the centrality of the church was discussed within the context of ethnic-Greeks of Asia Minor specifically, it was and remains to be central to many Greek-Americans.

For many Greek immigrants the church was a place to gather among those who shared a common culture and heritage, and as a result became the channel through which Greek Americans began to preserve the Hellenic identity.[256] As such, Hellenism in the United States and the Greek Orthodox Church became intertwined. Together they "served as the cord that kept the immigrant attached to the mother country" and helped preserve the "faith and language" of his forefathers.[257] This was done through the establishment of Greek-language schools. These programs which took place after school hours during the week, were offered by church communities in an effort to "perpetuate the modern Greek language" and to preserve the heritage

---

[255] *About the Greek Orthodox Archdiocese of America*, Greek Orthodox Archdiocese of America, http://www.goarch.org/about, accessed March 2018.
[256] Saloutos, *The Greeks in the United States*, 85–95.
[257] Saloutos, 122.

and identity of children born of Greek parents in the U.S.[258] In addition to this, communities formed fraternal societies that are equally a part of Greek American community life as Greek-language schools. These local *topika,* or societies, were numerous and varied based on the distinct make-up of each Greek community.[259]

Each Greek community in the United States is made up of Greek Americans descended from all across Greece. Descendants of the Greek Genocide are from Asia Minor which includes Pontos. The Pontic people come from villages in the Pontic Mountains that border the Black Sea in Asia Minor. They had a distinct language/dialect/culture, and for this reason they are distinguished as a separate group. This is reflected in the fact that there are *topika* dedicated to both Asia Minor and Pontos or just Pontos.

Of the groups that identify as specifically as Pontian societies, there are fifteen in the U.S. and Canada which are overseen by the Pan-Pontian Federation of U.S.A. and Canada established in 1980.[260] Each organization's activity is determined by the volunteers in each community and as such their impact can vary. That being said, the majority of the Pontian organizations are in the Northeastern and Midwestern US, with the highest concentrations of Pontic or Asia Minor descendants being in either New York or Chicago. As a result, the largest and most active organizations are both based in Chicago. These

---

[258] Saloutos, 72–73.
[259] Saloutos, 75.
[260] *Member Clubs,* Efxinos Pontos, http://www.efxinospontos.org/panpontian.html, accessed March 10, 2018,.

organizations are the Pontian Greek Society of Chicago and the Asia Minor and Pontos Hellenic Research Center.

The Pontian Greek Society of Chicago (formerly known as Xeniteas Pontian Society of Chicago) was founded in November of 1977 by Pontian Greek immigrants from Russia. Their founders were "determined to preserve the rich heritage that was passed down to them from their parents and grandparents, who were expelled from their homeland." To achieve this they do a number of things, most importantly they

- Collect, preserve and make use of historical documentation highlighting the Pontian Greek experience in Asia Minor and the Diaspora.
- Organize lectures and conferences devoted to illuminating the history of our people and the fate of the Greeks of the Diaspora today.
- Prepare and distribute educational materials for secondary schools and colleges and provide speakers to educational and civic organizations on Pontian Greek and Asia Minor history.
- Support the annual Day of Remembrance of the Pontian Greek Genocide and work to obtain proclamations, resolutions, and recognition of the genocide of Pontian Greeks from government entities.

- Host social events, such as dinner dances, to renew and preserve our historical traditions and practices.[261]

The challenge faced by descendants here in the U.S. is that there is not much material available in English. More challenging still, Greeks from Pontos spoke the Pontian dialect and others from Asia Minor generally spoke a dialect of Greek called Cappadocian—both of which are almost extinct.[262] In an effort to make research and education easier the PGSC has published oral histories, Pontic poems, information on traditional dance and histories in English.[263] By publishing all of this information not only online, but by also distributing it to educational institutions the PGSC has taken an active role in the international effort to educate the public in order to get the Greek Genocide recognized.

The most active and academic organization in the United States is the Asia Minor and Pontos Research Center, founded in 2011 as a 501 (c) non-profit organization in Chicago. Their goal is to "document and disseminate information about the Greek communities of the later Ottoman empire and study the expulsion of the Greeks from their ancestral homelands in Asia Minor (or

---

[261] *About the Pontian Greek Society*, Pontian Greek Society of Chicago, http://www.pontiangreeks.org/about-us/, accessed March 2018.
[262] *The Pontian Dialect*, Pontian Greek Society of Chicago, http://www.pontiangreeks.org/history/dialect, accessed March 2018.
[263] *History*, Pontian Greek Society of Chicago, http://www.pontiangreeks.org/history, accessed March 2018.

Anatolia), Eastern Thrace and Pontos."[264] This organization's focus on the multiple areas that were affected by the Genocide in Turkey is what makes them unique, as is their dedication to publication of all scholarship in the English language. Further, the AMPHRC works in conjunction with both Armenian and Jewish scholars in order to understand the framework within which the Greek Genocide occurs and is studied. AMPHRC is also the organization which, in conjunction with the Pan-Pontian Association of the USA and Canada, hosted the three academic conferences from 2008-2010 (these were the basis of Shirinian's publication in 2012). Additionally, they have hosted two international academic conferences in May 2013 and 2015. The AMPHRC provides invaluable information to the English-speaking researcher. They have archive and an online-searchable research library, they have a selected list of secondary sources and links to primary source newspaper articles. They even have teaching guides available for high school and elementary age students. The recent establishment of the research library was done in an effort to "attract the world's leading scholars," as is the organization of national and international academic research conferences.[265] The research and publications that are sponsored AMPHRC and other organizations are pushing to make more information available in English to make sure that more academic research can be published,

---

[264] *About us,* Asia Minor and Pontos Hellenic Research Center, http://www.hellenicresearchcenter.org/about, accessed March 2018.
[265] *Home,* Asia Minor and Pontos Hellenic Research Center, http://www.hellenicresearchcenter.org, accessed March 2018.

and to aid in the international recognition of the Greek
Genocide. While this type of preservation and study is
important equally important is the preservation of cultural
practices such as traditional dance.

    In the following section a survey of important
organizations pertaining to both Asia Minor and Pontos are
represented. It would seem from the survey provided here,
that they are the only organizations in the United States,
this is not the case. This is only a snapshot of hundreds of
organizations that exist across the U.S. are represent
immigrant communities from across Greece including but
not limited to Crete, Greeks of Egypt, Macedonia and
Thrace. While all members of these various associations
identify themselves as Greeks first, they also secondarily
identify as Cretan/Thracian/Macedonian. In fact, many
would first identify themselves in the opposite way—for
example Cretan first and then Greek. This is representative
of the distinct local cultures that pertain to specific regions
in Greece. Further, it should be noted that while many of
these organizations operate out of Greek Orthodox
Churches, not all Greeks are Christians. Some are Jewish or
even Muslim, but share the same culture and language
based on where their families are from. For example, the
Macedonian and Thracian Region there are still remnants
of the hybrid heterogenous culture mixing (discussed in
chapter 2) evident in the hybrid language that traditional
songs are sung, and the presence of identical dances across
Greece's northern shared borders. Ultimately, the
organizations discussed above and the dances that will be
discussed in the following section should be viewed as a

way to understand the nature of Asia Minor Greek cultural preservation in the U.S., but not as a comprehensive survey of all existing organizations.

Traditional Dance and Music

Traditional Greek Folk Dance is a cultural practice that can be traced back to before Christianity and through modern times. Mosaic murals depicting dance scenes can be found in ancient ruins across Greece and is a testament to the centrality of dance to their culture. After the adoption of Christianity by the Greek people dance continued to be a part of community life, and was common at social gatherings such as weddings, baptisms, funerals and more. There are a few references to dance, as a means of worship, in the bible mainly in the book of Psalms. Psalms 30:11 states that "for me my mourning [has turned] into dancing," and later in Psalms 150:4 Christians are prompted to "praise him with the timbrel and dance...with stringed instruments and organs."[266] Traditional dance became especially active during the Ottoman occupation from the fifteenth century to the beginning of the nineteenth century, as a way to maintain their unique Hellenic culture and identity.[267] In an effort to better understand the significance of traditional Greek dance, an analysis of the dance of Zolongo as well as the styling and symbolism of dances from Pontos will serve as a case study of the all dances that are native to Asia Minor and Greece.

To the Greeks, traditional dance was more than a simple activity done for enjoyment, it was a way to express their emotions, whatever they were. An example of this, is

---

[266] *King James Bible*, 10th ed. (Lisle, IL: Project Gutenberg, 1992).
[267] Solon Michaelides, "Greek Song-Dance," *Journal of the Interntional Folk Music Council* 8 (1956): 38.

the now famous stand taken by the women of the village Souli, Epirus in 1804. At the time the Turks were spreading throughout the peninsula, and Souli knew that they would be invaded. The women of the town decided that

> in order to avoid slavery and shame, hand-in hand
> with their children formed a circle and began
> dancing around the precipice singing a sad farewell
> song. When the leader of the circle reached the
> brink of the precipice she separated herself from
> the rest and fell to her death; then followed, after
> each verse, the second, the third until all [women
> and children] had perished.[268]

The "Dance of Zolongo," as it is now commonly known, has come to represent the struggle of freedom that the Greeks endured during the occupation of the Ottoman Empire and the Turks. The practice of traditional dance then became "a kind of cultural knowledge and performance, as a language of communication, embodied speech and embodied memories" of the various regions and villages of Hellenic origin[269].
. All Greek dances are performed in a semi-circle either holding hands or shoulders. Pontic dances though performed this way today, originally were done in a closed circle. There was no beginning or end of the line and served as a "symbol of bonding and union" that united the whole

---

[268] Michaelides, 38.
[269] Philia Issari, "Greek American Ethnic Identity, Cultural Experience and the 'Embodied Language' of Dance: Implications for Counseling," *International Journal for the Advancement of Counselling* 33, no. 4 (December 2011): 254.

community from children to elderly.[270] Pontic dances also reveal the effects of Turkish violence, as many of them are "militant in style, especially towards Eastern Pontos and the coastline." According to dance instructor and Pontic descendant Paul Calzada there are an estimated 10,000 traditional dances in Greece, with over 4,000 of those being unique to particular villages and regions. Pontos is estimated to have had approximately 3,500 dances of their own—many of which are lost today due to the genocide. Today, around 100 Pontic dances have been recovered, with the last ten being discovered by Nikos Zournadzidis in his travels to the area.[271]

As stated previously, dances from Pontos are danced in a circle which is similar to how dances from the varying regions in Greece are performed. While many Pontic dances are performed in closed circle, some are performed in a semi-circle, or a straight line. In many Greek dances where the societies were "more open [and] individualistic," the leader is able to perform special *figoures* or variations at the front of the line to show off to the community.[272] This was not/is not the case in Pontic dances. In dances from this region

> there is no lead dancer, no protagonist...everyone
> participates as an equal. The disciplined group of
> dancers...moves as one...Each Pontian bears the

---

[270] Philia Issari, "Greek American Ethnic Identity," *International Journal for the Advancement of Counselling* 33, no. 4 (December 2011): 261.

[271] Paul Calzada, Greek Genocide Survivor Descendants Interview, Transcript, January 17, 2018.

[272] Marianna Koromila, *The Greeks and The Black Sea: From the Bronze Age to the Early 20th Century* (Athens: Panorama Cultural Society, 2002), 247.

same burden of responsibility…A wrong step by the
third dancer or a slight hesitation by the sixth would
immediately mar the overall effect. The Pontian's
attitude to dance is the same as their attitude to
everyday life, where the entire village is responsible
for the community's survival. No one follows, and
no one leads.[273]

In effect, Pontian dances show the interconnectedness of
community members and its importance as a "ritual of
social reproduction and sustenance."[274] Their dances also
worked to visually embody and thus preserve the Pontic
community's memory and history. The same holds true for
the organizations here in the U.S. that are dedicated to the
preservation of Pontian memory and history. By teaching
each new generation the lyrics and dances of Greek and
Pontic culture, descendants are honoring the memory of the
ancestors who survived such great tragedy. As each move
is deliberate and representative of something, dancers are
physically embodying the memories and emotions that the
dances were created to express.

In the United States, the effort to maintain
traditional Greek dancing began as soon as immigrants
arrived. In the beginning churches performed and taught a
handful of dances that were common all across Greece such
as the Kalamatiano, Zembehiko and Hasaposeviko.
Independent organizations, like Pontic societies, focused on

[273] Koromila, 247.
[274] Issari, "Greek American Ethnic Identity, Cultural Experience and the 'Embodied
Language' of Dance: Implications for Counseling," 255.

teaching and learning dances from the regions that they trying to preserve. In essence, Macedonian societies learned and performed dances from Macedonia, Cretan societies from the island of Crete, and Pontic societies from the region of Pontos. By the end of the 1970s a group of Greek Orthodox Christians in California piloted the idea of a Greek dance competition where groups could showcase and present what they learned. The first two competitions, now known as the Greek Orthodox Folk Dance and Choral Festival, took place in 1976 and 1978 in the Metropolis of San Francisco. After its initial success, FDF was officially chartered in February of 1979 and has taken place every year in California, drawing over one thousand dancers, instructors, musicians and spectators from abroad.[275]

FDF is one of two major traditional Greek dance competitions in the U.S.; the second being the Hellenic Dance Festival (HDF). FDF's mission is to "promote, encourage and perpetuate Greek heritage and culture" in the forms of folk dance, folk art, music and language[276] HDF takes place on the east coast in the Metropolis of Atlanta, and was established in 2000. Similar to FDF, HDF looks to "bring Orthodox families together through dance, music and fellowship to perpetuate our rich Hellenic Orthodox Tradition" in order to "maintain our identity as Hellenes" and to "develop awareness and

---

[275] *Mission Statement,* Greek Orthodox Folk Dance and Choral Festival, http://www.yourfdf.org/pages/mission-statement/, accessed March 2018.
[276] *Mission Statement,* Greek Orthodox Folk Dance and Choral Festival, http://www.yourfdf.org/pages/mission-statement/, accessed March 2018.

appreciation...through dance and music."[277] Both competitions aim to preserve the rich traditional dance and music of Greece. This becomes even more evident based on the criterion used to judge groups. Rather than being judged based on synchronization or innovation of choreography groups are judged on authenticity. They are judged on how authentic and accurate their performance is compared to the village/region they are representing. Essentially, groups are not competing against each other, they are competing against the villages themselves.[278] Dance groups in the U.S. perform suites from all across Greece, but many groups choose to perform dances from the regions in northern Greece and what are now other Balkan nations. For example, dances from Thrace (north-eastern Greece) are very similar to dances that can be found across the border in Bulgaria and Turkey, because of the fluid nature of these culture prior to the creation of modern borders. In these competitions dances from Pontos are commonly performed by communities with large Pontic populations or with societies that sponsor them. Pontic dances are highly complex to perform and are known as war-like dances that represent their culture and struggle. As such, to watch a performance of Pontic dances can be an extremely evocative and emotional experience.

The most popular Pontic dances are those that are war-like in nature. All dances from this region are

---

[277] *Mission and Values*, Hellenic Dance Festival, https://www.hellenicdancefestival.com/mission-and-values/, accessed March 2018.
[278] *Mission and Values*, Hellenic Dance Festival, https://www.hellenicdancefestival.com/mission-and-values/, accessed March 2018.

performed using two instruments; the Pontic *lyra* and the *daouli* (pictured below). The *lyra* (left image) is a long and rectangular string instrument that is played on the musician's knee and with a bow, while the *daouli* (right image) is a large circular drum that is strapped to the shoulder.

279

When played together these instruments produce a heavy and warlike sound that is reflective of the region's struggle against Turkey in the nineteenth and twentieth centuries. The heavy and steady drum beat is reminiscent of war drums played when marching into battle while the high pitched upbeat rhythm of *lyra* emulates the chaotic nature of it. One of the oldest and most popular dances that embodies this is called the *Serra* or *Lazikon*. This ancient

---

[279] Christos Bairaktaris playing lyra in traditional dress, from the collection of Domna Samiou, ca. 1940s, accessed March 2018, http://www.karalahana.com/2015/10/25/well-known-pontian-kemence-players-videos-from-greece/; GreekReporter.com, *Untitled*, GreeksNet, December 2017, accessed March 2018, http://greeksnet.com/index.php/en/top-news-en/177-13-2-1.

war dance is still danced today in Pontos and is known as *Horon* or *Horonu*.

ΙΣΤΟΡΙΑ ΤΟΥ ΠΟΝΤΟΥ · ΛΑΪΚΟΣ ΧΟΡΟΣ   1985

HELLAS
ΕΛΛΗΝΙΚΗ ΔΗΜΟΚΡΑΤΙΑ   12

[280]

This challenging and dramatic dance was analyzed by P. Mouzenidis in the "Pontiaki Estia" periodical in 1956. Mouzenidis contends that the dance has three distinct parts depicting the stages Pontians as a community endured during the attacks of the Turks. In the first part dancers hold hands and raise their arms above their heads expressing a "mood of joy," this gradually fades into the second part where the dancers expression turns to one of "unease and the dancers' bodies [begin to] increase intensity their hands moving rhythmically forward and then backward."[281] The chaotic nature of the second part is meant to imitate "an injured fighter [that is] trying to cling

---

[280] Greek stamp "Story of Pontos," ca. 1985, PontosWorld, https://www.pontosworld.com/index.php/music/dances/586-the-serra.
[281] *Mission and Values*, Hellenic Dance Festival, https://www.hellenicdancefestival.com/mission-and-values/, accessed March 2018.

to life and to win." As the body is leaning over dancers make "small energetic and sudden movements [to] show [that] the wounded fighter is trying to survive." Finally, in the third phase "redemption arrives" and is depicted as the dancers once hunched over body "gains strength and…begins to jump up with his legs spread wide apart." The dancer's body then becomes "erect like a column and his head is held up with pride."[282] Thus displaying for all to see the struggle and triumph of the Pontic people in their battle to survive persecution and preserve their culture.

[282] Mouzenidis, P. *Dances The Serra,* PontosWord, https://www.pontosworld.com/index.php/music/dances/586-the-serra, accessed March 2018.

Conclusions: Right to Remember

Those who survived the Genocide of the Greeks, like the survivors of the Armenian Genocide and later the Holocaust, often seek to forget and commonly did not speak of the atrocities they both witnessed and endured, for many years. Survivors often seek to forget simply because it is painful to remember, or in other cases "because they are convinced that no one will listen respectfully to their stories" and so they work on moving forward and building new lives.[283] This coupled with the continued denial by both the Turkish Government and scholars who either deny or prefer the label ethnic cleansing serves to suffocate remembrance. This denial not only silences the voice of victims but sends the message that crimes against humanity bear no real consequence and so does not help prevent future atrocities but invites them to recur.[284]

Forgetting can be combatted by survivors and descendants demanding the right to remember. In Greece this has taken the form of monuments that are "rooted in the notion of identity" and dedicated to the "lost homelands" of their ancestors.[285] These monuments represent not only the "right to remember," but also the "duty of remembrance," which ensures that the memory of

---

[283] Jones, *Genocide: A Comprehensive Introduction*, 350.

[284] Jones, 356.

[285] Michel Bruneau and Kyriakos Papoulidis, "Remembering the Genocide of the 'Unforgettable Homelands:' The Erection of Commemorative Monuments in Greece by the Refugees of Asia Minor," in *The Genocide of the Ottoman Greeks: Studies in State-Sponsored Campaign of Extermination of the Christians of Asia Minor, 1912-1922 and Its Aftermath: History, Law, Memory* (Aristide D. Caratzas, 2011), 351.

the atrocities endured and the "heroism" of the victims who died, lives on.[286] All victims of oppression or violence must have the *right* to remember in order to heal and move forward. The denial of genocide withdraws a victim's right to remember, and declares experience of the oppressed as invalid, not worthy of remembrance, recognition or discussion. The right to remember their tragic pasts helps victims assimilate to their new communities while also, helping them to heal and move forward. When the wider community is actively aware of and involved in remembering, forgetting is not possible and as such validates the experiences of victims.

Here in the U.S. preservation of memory/remembrance is distinctly different than in Greece. Most of the Greeks of Asia Minor and Pontos that were survivors of the Genocide first immigrated to Greece, Russia or other European nations--it was their children who moved to the U.S. While there is more information available specifically pertaining to the Greek and Pontic Genocide in Greece, internationally there is less available in the English language, and as such has stagnated its research and recognition. As organizations like the AMPHRC begin to amass translated resources and publish scholarly sources, the right to remember in the U.S. has started to gain traction. This however is reflective only of acknowledgement of those outside the Greek community. As shown in this paper, survivors have utilized the Greek Orthodox church and independent organizations to

---

[286] Bruneau and Papoulidis, 352.

perpetuate and preserve the rich culture of their ancestors in Asia Minor and Pontos.

Through preservation and performance of traditional dance, music and the teaching of differing dialects, survivors ensure that their families and communities do not forget what was endured by their ancestors at the hands of the Turks. The collective memory, the memory of a group of people, of the Asia Minor and Pontic Greeks in America profoundly effects on how they experience the world around them. Their collective memory or their internal systems of belief, shape how they view and understand the world. It has had an impact on how they define and understand history, and how they fit into the broader national collective memory. By acknowledging their history and all they as a people were forced to endure, we can come to a common understanding of the past that encourages healing and prevents such atrocities as this from occurring again.

Truthfully, reading, rereading and analyzing the survivor testimonies and accounts of all the atrocities that occurred in Nicomedia was mentally, emotionally and even physically taxing. As such, I commend the many genocide scholars across all disciplines that have dedicated much of their lives to telling the stories of survivors. Their research and advocacy in both national and international theaters has assisted in the fight for recognition of victims so that atrocities such as this do not happen again. Despite all of the terrible things documented by Kostas Faltaits in his interviews with survivors, I did find heartening snippets throughout. I've come to think of them as moments of faith.

For example, in Ortakioy, a group of young girls were tied to the back of Giaour Ali's horse and dragged to the outskirts of town where he planned to kill them. Paraskevi Anastasiadou explained, that as soon as Ali raised his rifle at the girls "God…made his horse excited and it started stomping around in circles," so he spared all fifteen of them. Anastasiadou survived both Ali, and later escaped from a Turkish brigand who had taken her. Anastasiadou remembers her mom reminding her that it is "God who protects us," through this, she found the strength survive by any means necessary.[287]

Finally, this analysis would not have been possible if it were not for the Greeks of Asia Minor who found the strength to survive and to reestablish their lives in Greece where they were relocated. While I have looked exclusively at the accounts of those in Nicomedia, their experience was not unique. This is a small snippet of the genocidal violence that was being committed against all Christian minorities including Anatolian and Pontic Greeks, Armenians and Assyrians all over Turkey from 1914-1923.

Surviving victims of this genocide of Anatolian and Pontic Greek descent settled generally in either Greece or Russia, and it was the next generation, the children of the survivors, the descendants, who immigrated to the United States. With their immigration, resilience and determination came the establishment of Orthodox churches, societies and organizations dedicated to preserving the culture, heritage

---

[287] Faltaits, *The Genocide of the Greeks,* 94–95.

and memory of their ancestors from Asia Minor and
Pontos.

    I am a second generation Greek American, and a
third generation descendant of the Greek Genocide. It was
my ancestors who were forced to flee the only country that
they had ever known and to reestablish their lives in a
foreign country—Greece. My grandparents then chose to
immigrate to North America in 1964. My grandmother was
a part of the Asia-Minor descendants who chose to
reestablish elements of their communities and to preserve
their culture and heritage here in the U.S., recognizing the
importance of doing so. When I was ten years old, my
grandmother, Helen Mavromatis, who was interviewed for
this paper, took me to see Thea Halo (author of *Not Even
My Name)* speak, she made sure to tell me about how our
family had suffered long before I could ever understand
what she was talking about. Then, once I finally understood
the weight of what our ancestors went through, she stood
by and guided me. I would love to say that my grandmother
was the only Greek, Asia Minor descendant that did this,
but she was and is not. I offer you the story of my journey
in an effort to illustrate what descendants of the Greek
Genocide have passed down to their children and
grandchildren. All in an effort to make sure that first we,
the descendants remember, and second, that we do not
allow the world to forget—with the hope that the world
may never see such an atrocity again.

BIBLIOGRAPHY

Agnew, John. "No Borders, No Nations: Making Greece in MAcedonia." *Annals of the Association of American Geographers* 97, no. 2 (June 2007): 398–422.

Akçam, Taner. "The Greek Deportations and Massacres of 1913-1914: A Trial Run for the Armenian Genocide." In *The Asia Minor Catastrophe and the Ottoman Greek Genocide: Essays on Asia Minor, Pontos, and Eastern Thrace, 1912-1923,* edited by George N. Shirinian, 69-88. Bloomingdale, IL: The Asia Minor and Pontos Research Center, INC, 2012.

Akçam, Tanner. *Young Turks' Crime.* (2012): 55, 97. Quoted in Erik Sjöberg, *The Making of the Greek Genocide.* New York: Berghahn, 2017.

Aksan, Virginia H. "Ottoman to Turk: Continuity and Change." *International Journal* 61, no. 1 (Winter /2006 2005): 19–38.

Asia Minor and Pontos Hellenic Research Center. "About Us." Accessed March 2018. http://www.hellenicresearchcenter.org/about.

Asia Minor and Hellenic Research Center. "Home."
Accessed March 2018.
http://www.hellenicresearchcenter.org.

Badiul Alam, Muhammad. "Contemporary Ideas and
Theories of Nationalism." *The Indian Journal of
Political Science* 41, no. 3 (September 1980): 367–
78.

Barton, James L. *"Turkish Atrocities": Statements of
American Missionaries on the Destruction of
Christian Communities in Ottoman Turkey, 1915-
1917.* Ann Arbor, MI: Gomidas Institute, 1998.

Baum, Steven K. *The Psychology of Genocide:
Perpetrators, Bystanders, and Rescuers.*
Cambridge: Cambridge University Press, 2008.

Bell-Fialkoff. "A Brief History of Ethnic Cleansing."
Foreign Affairs 72, no. 3 (Summer 1993): 110-121.
Accessed February 2018.

Bjørnlund, Matthias. "Danish Sources on the Destruction of
the Ottoman Greeks, 1914-1916." In *The Genocide
of the Ottoman Greeks: Studies on the State-
sponsored Campaign of Extermination of the
Christians of Asia Minor, 1912-1922 and Its
Aftermath: History, Law, Memory,* edited by Tessa
Hofmann, Matthias Bjørnlund, and Vasileios

Meichanetsidis, 137-178. New York: Aristide D. Caratzas, 2011.

Bjørnlund, Matthias. "The Persecution of Greeks and Armenians in Smyrna, 1914-1916: A Special Case in the Course of the Late Ottoman Genocides. In *The Asia Minor Catastrophe and the Ottoman Greek Genocide: Essays on Asia Minor, Pontos, and Eastern Thrace, 1912-1923,* edited by George N. Shirinian, 89-134. Bloomingdale, IL: The Asia Minor and Pontos Research Center, INC, 2012.

Brubaker, Rogers. "Ethnicity, Race, and Nationalism." *Annual Review of Sociology* 35 (2009): 21–42.

Bruneau, Michel and Kiriakos Papoulidis. "Remembering the Genocide and the 'Unforgettable Homelands:' The Erection of Commemorative Monuments in Greece by the Refugees of Asia Minor." In *The Genocide of the Ottoman Greeks: Studies on the State-sponsored Campaign of Extermination of the Christians of Asia Minor, 1912-1922 and Its Aftermath: History, Law, Memory,* edited by Tessa Hofmann, Matthias Bjørnlund, and Vasileios Meichanetsidis, 351-370. New York: Aristide D. Caratzas, 2011.

Chalk, Frank and Kurt Jonassohn. *The History and Sociology of Genocide.* New Haven, CT: Yale University Press, 2002.

Charny, Israel W. *The Encyclopedia of Genocide.* Santa
    Barbara: ABC-CLIO, 1999.

Charny, Israel W. "The Integrity and Courage to Recognize
    All the Victims of a Genocide." In *The Genocide of*
    the Ottoman Greeks: Studies on the State-sponsored
    Campaign of Extermination of the Christians of
    Asia Minor, 1912-1922 and Its Aftermath: History,
    Law, Memory, edited by Tessa Hofmann, Matthias
    Bjørnlund, and Vasileios Meichanetsidis, 21-38.
    New York: Aristide D. Caratzas, 2011.

Clark, Bruce. *Twice a stranger: Greece, Turkey and the*
    minorities they expelled. London: Granta, 2005.

Clogg, Richard. *A Concise History of Greece.* Cambridge:
    Cambridge University Press, 1992.

Cooper, Allan D. *The Geography of Genocide.* Lanham:
    University Press of America, 2009.

Coufoudakis, Van. "From Lausanne (1923) to Cyprus
    (2009): Turkey's Violations of International Law
    and the Destruction of Historic Hellenic
    Communities." In *The Asia Minor Catastrophe and*
    the Ottoman Greek Genocide: Essays on Asia
    Minor, Pontos, and Eastern Thrace, 1912-1923,
    edited by George N. Shirinian, 249-272.

Bloomingdale, IL: The Asia Minor and Pontos Research Center, INC, 2012.

Cox, John M. *To Kill a People: Genocide in the Twentieth Century.* New York: Oxford University Press, 2017.

Dadrian, Vahakn N. "A Typology of Genocide." *International Review of Modern Sociology* 5 no. 2 (1975): 201-212.

Das, Veena. "Collective Violence and the Shifting Categories of Communal Riots, Ethnic Cleansing and Genocide." In *The Historiography of Genocide,* edited by Dan Stone, 93-127. New York, NY: Palgrave Macmillian, 2008.

de Zayas, Alfred. "The Ottoman Genocide of the Greeks and the Other Christian Minorities in Light of the Genocide Convention." In *The Genocide of the Ottoman Greeks: Studies on the State-sponsored Campaign of Extermination of the Christians of Asia Minor, 1912-1922 and Its Aftermath: History, Law, Memory,* edited by Tessa Hofmann, Matthias Bjørnlund, and Vasileios Meichanetsidis, 211-340. New York: Aristide D. Caratzas, 2011.

Der Krikorian, Abraham and Eugene Taylor. "Achieving Ever-Greater Precision in Attestation and Attribution of Genocide Photographs." In *The Genocide of the Ottoman Greeks: Studies on the*

State-sponsored Campaign of Extermination of the Christians of Asia Minor, 1912-1922 and Its Aftermath: History, Law, Memory, edited by Tessa Hofmann, Matthias Bjørnlund, and Vasileios Meichanetsidis, 389-434. New York: Aristide D. Caratzas, 2011.

Dixon, Jennifer M. "Defending the Nation? Maintaining Turkey's Narrative of the Armenian Genocide," *South European Society and Politics* 15:3(2010): 467-485. Accessed March 29, 2017.

Dobkin, Marjorie Housepian. *Smyrna 1922: The Destruction of a City.* 4th ed. New York: Newmark Press, 1998.

Donef, Racho. "The Role of Teşkilât-I Mahsua (Special Organization)." In *The Genocide of Ottoman Greeks: Studies in State-Sponsored Campaign of Extermination of the Christians of Asia Minor, 1912-1922 and Its Aftermath: History, Law, Memory,* edited by Tessa Hofmann, Matthias Bjørnlund, and Vasileios Meichanetsidis, 179-194. New York: Aristide D. Caratzas, 2011.

Dragostinova, Theodora. "Continuity vs. Radical Break: National Homogenization campaigns in the Greek-Bulgarian borderlands before and after the Balkan Wars." *Journal of Genocide Research* 18, no. 4 (October 2016): 405-426.

Editors of Encyclopedia Britannica. "Alexander."
    Encyclopedia Britannica. Accessed March 2018.
    http://www.britannica.com/biography/Alexander-
    king-of-Greece.

Efxinos Pontos. "Member Clubs." Accessed March 10,
    2018.
    http://www.efxinopontos.org/panpontian.html.

Eltringham, Nigel. *Remembering Genocide.* Abingdon:
    Routledge, 2014.

Faltaits, Kostas, Ellene S. Phufas-Jousma, and Aris
    Tsilfidis. *The Genocide of the Greeks in Turkey:
    Survivor Testimonies from the Nicomedia (Izmit)
    Massacres of 1920-1921.* River Vale, New Jersey:
    Cosmos Publishing, an Imprint of Attica Editions,
    2016.

Fein, Helen. "Genocide and Other State Murders in the
    Twentieth Century." Lecture at the Holocaust
    Memorial Museum, Washington, D.C., October 24,
    1995.

Fein, Helen. "Genocide: A Sociological Perspective." In
    Genocide: An Anthropological Reader edited by
    Alexander Laban Hinton, 74-90. Malden: Blackwell
    Publishers, 2002.

Gellner, Ernest. *Nations and Nationalism*. Oxford: Blackwell, 1983.

George Palaidis, interview by Elenie Louvaris, Greek Genocide Survivor Descendants Interview, Transcript, March 7, 2018.

Greek Orthodox Archdiocese of America. "About the Greek Orthodox Archdiocese of America." Accessed March 2018. http://www.goarch.org/about.

Greek Orthodox Folk Dance and Choral Festival. "Mission Statement." Accessed March 2018. http://www.yourfdf.org/pages/mission-statement/.

Halo, Thea. *Not Even My Name: From a Death March in Turkey to a New Home in America, a Young Girl's True Story of Genocide and Survival*. New York: Picador USA, 2000.

Hanioglu, M. Şükrü. *Atatürk: an intellectual biography*. Princeton: Princeton University Press, 2011.

Hatzidimitriou, Constantine. "The Destruction of Smyrna in 1922: American Sources and Turkish Responsibility." In *The Asia Minor Catastrophe and the Ottoman Greek Genocide,* edited by George N. Shirinian, 155-229. Bloomingdale: The Asia Minor and Pontos Research Center INC, 2012.

Hayes, Peter. *How was it Possible? A Holocaust reader.*
Lincoln: University of Nebraska Press, 2015.

Helen Mavromatis, interview by Elenie Louvaris, audio
recording, Family and Personal History, April 3,
2017.

Hellenic Dance Festival. "Mission and Values." Accessed
March 2018.
http://www.hellenicdancefestival.com/mission-and-
values/.

Herman, Edward S. and David Peterson. *The Politics of
Genocide.* New York: Monthly Review Press, 2010.

Hinton, Alexander Laban. *Genocide: An Anthropological
Reader.* Malden: Blackwell, 2002.

Hirsch, Herbert. *Genocide and the Politics of Memory:
Studying Death to Preserve Life.* Chapel Hill:
University of North Carolina Press, 1995.

Hirschon Renée. *Heirs of the Greek Catastrophe: The
Social Life of Asia Minor Refugees in Piraeus.*
Oxford: Berghahn Books, 1989.

Hofmann, Tessa, Matthias Bjørnlund, and Vasileios
Meichanetsidis. *The Genocide of the Ottoman
Greeks: Studies on the State-sponsored Campaign*

*of Extermination of the Christians of Asia Minor,
1912-1922 and Its Aftermath: History, Law,
Memory.* New York: Aristide D. Caratzas, 2011.

Hofmann, Tessa. "Γενοκτονία Εν Ροή: Cumulative
Genocide the Massacres and Deportations of the
Greek Population of the Ottoman Empire (1912-
1923)." In *The Genocide of the Ottoman Greeks:
Studies on the State-sponsored Campaign of
Extermination of the Christians of Asia Minor,
1912-1922 and Its Aftermath: History, Law,
Memory,* edited by Tessa Hofmann, Matthias
Bjørnlund, and Vasileios Meichanetsidis, 39-112.
New York: Aristide D. Caratzas, 2011.

International Association of Genocide Scholars. "IAGS-
Resolution-Assyrian and Greek Genocide."
Resolutions. Accessed September 14, 2016.
http://www.genocidescholars.org/resources/resoluti
ons.

Issari, Philia. "Greek American Ethnic Identity, Cultural
Experience and the 'Embodied Language' of
Dance: Implications for Counseling." *International
Journal for the Advancement of Counselling* 33, no.
4 (December 2011): 261.

Jacobs, Steven Leonard. "Genocide of Others: Raphael
Lemkin, The Genocide of the Greeks, the
Holocaust, and the Present Moment." In *The*

Genocide of the Ottoman Greeks: Studies in State-Sponsored Campaign of Extermination of the Christians of Asia Minor, 1912-1922 and Its Aftermath: History, Law, Memory, 297-310. New York: Aristide D. Caratzas, 2011.

Jones, Adam. *Genocide: A Comprehensive Introduction.* New York: Routledge, 2006.

Jones, Adam. *Genocide, War Crimes and the West: History and Complicity.* London: Zed Books, 2013.

Karagianis, Lydia. *Smoldering Smyrna.* New York: Carlton Pr, 1996.

Kitroeff, Alexander. "Asia Minor Refugees in Greece: A History of Identity and Memory, 1920s-1980s." In *The Asia Minor Catastrophe and the Ottoman Greek Genocide,* edited by George N. Shirinian, 229-248. Bloomingdale: The Asia Minor and Pontos Research Center INC, 2012.

Korb, Alexander. "Homogenizing Southeastern Europe, 1912-99: Ethnic Cleansing in the Balkans Revisited," *Journal of Genocide Research* 18:4 (2016): 377-387. Accessed December 2, 2016

Koromila, Marianna, *The Greeks and the Black Sea: From the Bronze Age to the Early 20th Century,* 247.

Athens: Panorama Cultural Society, 2002.
http://pontiangreeks.org/history/dances/.

Lemarchand, Rene. *Forgotten Genocides: oblivion, denial, and memory.* Philadelphia: University of Pennsylvania Press, 2011.

Levitsky, Ronald. "Teaching the Greek Genocide." In *The Genocide of the Ottoman Greeks: Studies on the State-sponsored Campaign of Extermination of the Christians of Asia Minor, 1912-1922 and Its Aftermath: History, Law, Memory,* edited by Tessa Hofmann, Matthias Bjørnlund, and Vasileios Meichanetsidis, 342-350. New York: Aristide D. Caratzas, 2011.

Malešević, Siniša. "Did Wars Make Nation-States in the Balkans?: Nationalisms, Wars and States in the 19th and Early 20th Century South East Europe." *Journal of Historical Sociology* 25, no. 3 (September 2012): 299–330.

Map of Asia Minor: Todays Turkey. English, Colour. Maps of Pontos and Pontic Region. http://www.angelfire.com/folk/pontian_net/map.html.

Mazower, Mark. *The Balkans: a Short History.* New York: Modern Library, 2000.

Mazower, Mark. *Salonica, City of Ghosts: Christians, Muslims, and Jews, 1430-1950.* New York: Alfred A. Knopf, 2005.

Michaelides, Solon. "Greek Song and Dance." *Journal of the International Folk Music Council* 8 (1956): 28.

Mourelos, John. "The 1914 Persecutions of Greeks in the Ottoman Empire and the First Attempt at an Exchange of Minorities between Greece and Turkey." In *The Genocide of the Ottoman Greeks: Studies on the State-sponsored Campaign of Extermination of the Christians of Asia Minor, 1912-1922 and Its Aftermath: History, Law, Memory,* edited by Tessa Hofmann, Matthias Bjørnlund, and Vasileios Meichanetsidis, 113-136. New York: Aristide D. Caratzas, 2011.

Mouzenidis, P. "Dances The Serra." PontosWorld. Accessed March 2018. http://www.pontosworld.com/index.php/music/dances/586-the-serra.

Naimark, Norman M. *Fires of Hatred: Ethnic Cleansing in Twentieth-Century Europe.* Cambridge, MA: Harvard University Press, 2001.

Özkirimli, Umut, and Steven Grosby. "Nationalism Theory Debate: The Antiquity of Nations?" *Nations and Nationalism* 13, no. 3 (2007): 523–37.

Papanikolas, Helen. *An Amulet of Greek Earth: Generations of Immigrant Folk Culture.* Athens: Swallow Press; Ohio University Press, 2002.

Papoutsky, Christos. *Ships of Mercy: The True Story of the Rescue of the Greeks, Smyrna, September 1922.* Portsmouth, NH: Peter Randall Pub, 2008.

Paul Calzada, interview by Elenie Louvaris, Greek Genocide Survivor Descendants Interview, Transcript, January 17, 2018.

Pontian Greek Society of Chicago. "About the Pontian Greek Society." Accessed March 2018. http://www.pontiangreeks.org/about-us/.

Pontian Greek Society of Chicago. "The Pontian Dialect." Accessed March 2018. http://www.pontiangreeks.org/history/dialect.

Pontian Greek Society of Chicago. "History." Accessed March 2018. http://www.pontiangreeks.org/history.

Pranger, Robert J. "U.S. Policy in Recognizing the Genocides of Christian Minorities in the Late Ottoman Empire: Challenges and Opportunities." In *The Asia Minor Catastrophe and the Ottoman Greek Genocide,* edited by George N. Shirinian,

273-290. Bloomingdale: The Asia Minor and
Pontos Research Center INC, 2012.

Psomiades, Harry J. "The American Near East Relief
    (NER) and the *Megale Katastrophe* in 1922." In
    *The Genocide of the Ottoman Greeks: Studies on
    the State-sponsored Campaign of Extermination of
    the Christians of Asia Minor, 1912-1922 and Its
    Aftermath: History, Law, Memory,* edited by Tessa
    Hofmann, Matthias Bjørnlund, and Vasileios
    Meichanetsidis, 265-276. New York: Aristide D.
    Caratzas, 2011.

Ratner, Steven R. and Jason S. Abrams. *Accountability for
    Human Rights Atrocities in International Law:
    Beyond the Nuremburg Legacy.* Oxford: Oxford
    University Press, 2001.

Robins, Nicholas A., and Adam Jones. *Genocides by the
    oppressed: subaltern genocide in theory and
    practice.* Bloomington: Indiana University Press,
    2009.

Ryan, Arthur C. "Statement of the Misrule of Turkey and
    Her Crule Treatment of Non-Moslem Subjects," in
    *"Turkish Atrocities:" Statements of American
    Missionaries on the Destruction of Christian
    Communities in Ottoman Turkey, 1915-1917,* edited
    by James L. Barton, 181. Ann Arbor: Gomidas
    Institute, 1998

Saloutos, Theodore. *The Greeks in the United States.* Cambridge: Harvard University Press, 1964.

Sandy Papadopoulos, interview by Elenie Louvaris, Greek Genocide Survivor Descendants Interview, Transcript, March 4, 2018.

Shaw, Martin. *What is Genocide?* Cambridge, UK: Polity Press, 2015.

Shirinian, George N. *The Asia Minor Catastrophe and the Ottoman Greek Genocide: Essays on Asia Minor, Pontos, and Eastern Thrace, 1912-1923.* Bloomingdale, IL: The Asia Minor and Pontos Research Center, INC, 2012.

Sjöberg, Erik. *The Making of the Greek Genocide: Contested Memories of the Ottoman Greek Catastrophe.* New York, NY: Berghahn Books, 2017.

Smith, Roger; Eric Markusen and Robert Jay Lifton. "Professional Ethics and the Denial of Armenian Genocide," *Holocaust and Genocide Studies* V9N1(1995): 1-22. Accessed March 29, 2017.

Stavridis, Stavros T. "International Red Cross: A Mission to Nowhere." In *The Genocide of the Ottoman Greeks: Studies on the State-sponsored Campaign of Extermination of the Christians of Asia Minor, 1912-1922 and Its Aftermath: History, Law, Memory,* edited by Tessa Hofmann, Matthias Bjørnlund, and Vasileios Meichanetsidis, 277-296. New York: Aristide D. Caratzas, 2011.

Stone, Dan. *The Historiography of Genocide.* New York: Palgrave Macmillian, 2008.

Tsirkinidis, Harry. *At Last We Uprooted Them: The Genocide of Greeks of Pontos, Thrace and Asia Minor through French Archives.* Translated by Stratos Mavrantonis. Thessaloniki, GR: Kyriakidis Brother Publishing House, 1999.

Talaat, "Secret Order of the Turkish Minster of Internal Affairs, Talaat, Dated 14th May, 1914." In *At Last We Uprooted Them,* edited by Harry Tsirkinidis, 107. Thessaloniki: Publishing House Kyriakkidis Brothers s.a., n.d.

Turlington, Edgar. "The Settlement of Lausanne." *The American Journal of International Law* 18, no. 4 (1924): 696. doi:10.2307/2188844.

Ülker, Erol. "Contextualizing 'Turkification': Nation-Building in the Late Ottoman Empire, 1908-18." *Nations and Nationalism* 11, no. 4 (2005): 613–36.

Üngör, Uğur Ümit. "Seeing like a Nation-State: Young Turk Social Engeineering in Eastern Turkey, 1913-50." *Journal of Genocide Research* 10, no. 1 (June 2008): 15–39.

Üngör, Uğur Ümit. *The Making of Modern Turkey: Nation and State in Eastern Anatolia, 1913-1950*. Oxford: Oxford University Press, 2011.

Üngör, Uğur Ümit. "Lost in Commemoration: the Armenian Genocide in Memory and Identity," *Patterns of Prejudice* 48:2 (2014): 147-166. Accessed March 29, 2017.

United Nations. "United Nations Office on Genocide Prevention and the Responsibility to Protect: Convention on the Prevention and Punishment of the Crime of Genocide." Accessed September 12, 2017. http://www.un.org/en/genocideprevention/genocide.html.

Urenekc, Lou. *Smyrna, September 1922: The American Mission to Rescue Victims of the 20th Century's First Genocide*. New York: Harper Collins, 2015.

Wactor, Olan. *Map of Nicomedia (Izmit) Region*. The Genocide Research Center. http://greek-genocide.net/index.php/component/content/article?id=269:the-genocide-of-the-greeks-in-turkey.

Made in the USA
Columbia, SC
19 November 2023

26754507R00086